Ninja Max XL Air Fryer Cookbook for Beginners

2000-Day Tasty and Easy Air Fryer Recipes for Cooking Easier, Faster, And More Enjoyable for You and Your Family!

Jime Yaem

Table of Contents

Introduction

With the Ninja Max XL Air Fryer Cookbook for Beginners, you can get the most from your Ninja air fryer to make a low-fat, and healthier way of cooking your favorite fried foods. The air fryer recipes equipped in this book was specially hand-picked and tried in our kitchen to produce near possible accurate results.

The most important part of this book is the hassle-free recipes, which give you a lot of choices for your breakfast, lunch, dinner, snack and dessert, etc. Not only will you find meat recipes, but also will find dishes for vegan & Vegetarians.

Chapter 1: Ninja Max XL Air Fryer Basics

Ninja Max XL Air Fryer: Cooks, Crips, Dehydrates

This 4 in one Air Fryer is known for its simplicity and elegant design. The machine is proven to be user friendly as it comes with a one-touch control panel and display screen. The modes are clearly indicated on the buttons, and the operation keys are also given around the display screen. The Power and Start/Pause buttons are given separately to operate the appliance.

Understanding the Appliance

With its high gloss finish in black, the 4 quarts Ninja Max XL Air Fryer add an elegant appeal to your kitchen outlook. It has this compact design, which makes it suitable for every other countertop, and the users can easily move the fryer from places to places with much ease and convenience. In this Air Fryer, you can enjoy four different cooking modes, which can be used at the desired temperature and timer settings.

Air Fry: This function allows you to cook super crispy and delicious food with 75 percent lesser use of oil than conventional frying.

Roast: The roasting mode allows the user to roast all the steaks, meat, poultry, veggies, nuts, and fruits at low, medium, and high temperatures.

Dehydrate: Through its dehydrating mode, the user can make meat jerkies, chips, and crisps.

Reheat: The Ninja Max XL Air Fryer can easily replace your conventional microwave because it can reheat your food at any desired temperature with the help of its reheat mode.

Features and Specs of the Ninja Max XL Air Fryer

The following are the major features of a Standard 4 Quart Ninja Max XL Air Fryer. There are a number of fryer models that are available in this size, and you can choose any according to your cooking requirements. Here are discussing the Ninja Max XL Air Fryer AF 101:

- BPA free:
- 4 quarts Capacity
- Black and Gray Color
- 2.6 Ft Cord length
- Dishwasher-safe Accessories

- 13.6 Length x 11 Width x 13.3 Heign in inches:
- Product weight: 10.58 lbs.
- Wattage: 1550 watts

Besides the basic cooking modes, the appliance also comes with the TIME and TEMP adjustment keys so that you could easily adjust the settings manually and cook however you want. The temperature of the appliance ranges from 105 degrees F to 400 degrees F. This range is enough to dehydrate some food at the lowest temperature and Air fry others on the highest temperatures.

How to Use a Ninja Max XL Air Fryer: Steps for Efficient Cooking

The 4-quart Ninja Max XL Air Fryer can be your best kitchen company if you regularly cook crispy snacks and desserts or if you like to roast delicious entrees. You can put this appliance to the best use by using it in the following step by step manner.

- **Start**

To begin cooking, first plugin the device. It is best to unplug it after every cooking session and only plug it in before the next session. In this way, you can prevent the chances of short circuits or save the device from any damage due to electricity fluctuations.

After plugging in the appliance, check if it's functioning and display screen lights up. Then remove the Air Fryer basket and wipe it with a clean cloth inside out. The accessories you are going to use to place the food inside must also be cleaned and washed properly.

- **Set the Appliance**

It's about time to put all the accessories and the Air Fryer basket back into the unit before you start the device for preheating. Make sure that the appliance is placed on a stable and sturdy surface. It should be at least 1 ft away from other appliances and heat sources, and the vent of the Air Fryer must not be covered in any way.

- **Preheat**

After inserting the basket into the unit, you need to select the mode you want to cook your food at. You can choose:

1. Roast
2. Air Fry
3. Dehydrate

Depending upon the recipe and the type of food you want to cook. When you press the desired function button, the display will automatically display a preset temperature and time that you can change according to the recipe requirement. And to change the cooking time, using the UP and DOWN keys for TIME to increase or decrease the cooking time. Remember that you need to add three additional minutes to actually cooking time in order to preheat the device.

Once the time is set, you can also adjust the temperature by using the UP and DOWN Temperature keys to increase or decrease the value.

- **Prepare**

While the appliance is preheating, make sure that your food is ready to be placed inside the Air Fryer basket. It is best to keep the food ready before preheating and setting the machine's mode, temperature, and time because Ninja Max XL Air Fryer, due to its effective heating technology, preheats quickly.

- **Initiate**

As soon as the appliance is preheated, pull out the basket, press the START/PAUSE button to stop the timer, and place the food inside the basket. Insert the basket back in the unit and press the START/PAUSE button to resume cooking. You can repeat this step to toss or flip the food during cooking.

Step by Step Cleaning

Cleaning is important for the maintenance of your appliance. Here is how you should do it:

1. Clean your Air Fryer after every last session of cooking.
2. Allow the appliance to cool down completely before you start cleaning.
3. Never start cleaning the appliance when it is still plugged in. Always unplug the appliance before cleaning.
4. Start cleaning by removing all the accessories from the unit. Remove the Air Fryer basket and other pans, racks, or jar placed inside for cooking.
5. The ceramic coated Air Fryer basket, the crisper plate, and other accessories are dishwasher safe and can be easily washed. Make sure not to scrub them with hard scrubbers.
6. The Air Fryer unit can be cleaned by wiping off its surfaces with a damp cloth.
7. Never immerse the Air Fryer unit and its power cord in the water, or any soap liquid.
8. Allow all the accessories and Air Fryer basket to dry before putting them back to their places.

Troubleshooting

There are certain errors and problems that may appear due to the mishandling of the appliance or lack of information. But don't worry! Such problems are fixable! And here is how you do it:

1. **Ingredients Blowing Around during Air Frying**

It happens due to a powerful fan of the Air Fryer, which blows air with pressure. To keep ingredients in place, take the necessary precautions like inserting a toothpick to keep the top slice of a sandwich in place or press the breading of the coat meat or snack.

2. **Air Fryer Temperature is not increasing**

The Ninja Max XL Air Fryer can only heat up to 400 degrees F. If the unit reaches the desired temperature, it will not heat any further. Cook the food inside this fryer according to its given temperature range.

3. **Display screen going black**

When the appliance goes into the Standby mode, it's display screen automatically turns black, and you can turn on the display by pressing the power button. The screen lights up again once the power is back on.

4. **"E" message on the display screen**

"E" stands for error, and it indicates that the appliance is having some technical difficulty in its proper functioning. Take this sign seriously and always contact the customer service of the Ninja Foodi and discuss the problem. It is best not to use the appliance until this problem is not resolved by the company's representatives.

5. **Unit not heating up**

The unit needs time to preheat before attaining the set cooking temperatures. For best results, it is recommended to preheat the unit before adding food to its basket. Allow the unit to preheat on its own, and once it reaches this temperature, it will stop heating up any further.

Frequently Asked Questions

It's not easy to get along with a newly bought cooking appliance; there are a number of details and functions that can only be learned after the hands-on experience. There are several questions that may pop up in your mind while using this Ninja Max XL Air Fryer, and here are the most relevant answers to your queries:

1. **Can we fry wet batter-coated food in the Air Fryer?**

Yes, but it is important to use proper technique for breading. Always coat foods first with flour, then dip in the egg, and then coat with the bread crumbs. So, the batter remains coated on the food. Make sure to lightly press the bread crumbs onto the food. Otherwise, the powerful fan of the Air Fryer can sometimes blow off the breading of the food. By pressing the crumbs firmly on, you can prevent that.

2. **Can we use aluminum foil and parchment paper in the basket?**

Yes, it is completely safe to use both the parchment paper sheet and aluminum foil in the basket. But only use these sheets when it is necessary.

3. **Do we need to shake the Air Fryer basket while cooking?**

Yes, for even browning and consistent crispiness, it is recommended to frequently check on and shake or toss your food by shaking the basket or with the help of the silicone-tipped tongs.

4. **Do we have to use cooking oil when air frying?**

No, the oil should not be used for Air Frying, but for some recipes, it is recommended. For instance, to Air Fry fresh vegetables, use about 1 tablespoon of oil to lightly grease veggies. A little oil is good to achieve a perfect level of crisp. For even browning, use an oil spray or spritzer to coat the ingredients evenly.

5. **Do we need to preheat the Air Fryer before cooking?**

Yes, for good results, it is recommended to preheat the appliance before adding the food to the basket. To preheat the unit, add 3 minutes extra to the actual cook time and let the unit reach the desired temperature.

6. **Do I need to pause the Air Fryer unit when I pull out its basket?**

Yes. When you simply pull the basket out of the Air Fryer, the timer continues to count down, and the fan continues to run. So, to pause the Air Fryer, press its START/PAUSE button and then to resume cooking again press this START/PAUSE BUTTON.

Chapter 2: Breakfast Recipes

French Toast

Preparation Time: 10 minutes
Cooking Time: 5 minutes
Servings: 2

Ingredients:

- 2 eggs
- ¼ cup evaporated milk
- 3 tablespoons sugar
- 2 teaspoons olive oil
- 1/8 teaspoon ground cinnamon
- 1/8 teaspoon vanilla extract
- 4 bread slices

Method:

1. Set the temperature of Ninja Max XL Air Fryer to 390 degrees F and select "Air Fry" to preheat for 5 minutes.
2. Grease an Air Fryer pan and insert in the Air Fryer while heating.
3. Press "Start/Pause" to begin.
4. In a large bowl, add all the ingredients except for bread slices and mix well.
5. Coat the bread slices with egg mixture evenly.
6. Press "Start/Pause" press "Start/Pause" to pause cooking and arrange the bread slices in the prepared pan.
7. Set the time for 5 minutes and Press "Start/Pause" to begin.
8. While cooking, flip the slices once halfway through.
9. Serve warm.

Nutritional Information per Serving:

- Calories 262
- Total Fat 12 g
- Saturated Fat 3.6 g
- Cholesterol 173 mg
- Sodium 218 mg
- Total Carbs 30.8 g
- Fiber 0.5 g
- Sugar 22.3 g
- Protein 9.1 g

Simple Bread

Preparation Time: 15 minutes
Cooking Time: 18 minutes
Servings: 4

Ingredients:

- 7/8 cup whole-wheat flour
- 7/8 cup plain flour
- 1¾ ounces pumpkin seeds
- 1 teaspoon salt
- ½ of sachet instant yeast
- ½-1 cup lukewarm water

Method:

1. In a bowl, mix together the flours, pumpkin seeds, salt and yeast and mix well.
2. Slowly, add the desired amount of water and mix until a soft dough ball forms.
3. With your hands, knead the dough until smooth and elastic.
4. Place the dough ball into a bowl.
5. With a plastic wrap, cover the bowl and set aside in a warm place for 30 minutes or until doubled in size.
6. Set the temperature of Ninja Max XL Air Fryer to 350 degrees F and select "Air Fry" to preheat for 5 minutes.
7. Press "Start/Pause" to begin.
8. Place the dough ball in a greased cake pan and brush the top of the dough with water.
9. Arrange the cake pan in the fryer basket.
10. Slide the basket in Air Fryer and select "Air Fry" for 18 minutes.
11. Press "Start/Pause" to begin.
12. Remove from Air Fryer and place the pan onto a wire rack for about 10-15 minutes.
13. Carefully, invert the bread onto the wire rack to cool completely cool before slicing.
14. Cut the bread into desired sized slices and serve.

Nutritional Information per Serving:

- Calories 268
- Total Fat 6 g
- Saturated Fat 1.1 g
- Cholesterol 0 mg
- Sodium 585 mg
- Total Carbs 43.9 g
- Fiber 2.5 g
- Sugar 1.1 g
- Protein 9.2 g

Sausage Frittata

Preparation Time: 10 minutes
Cooking Time: 10 minutes
Servings: 1

Ingredients:

- ½ of Italian sausage, sliced
- 4 cherry tomatoes, halved
- 3 eggs
- 1 tablespoon olive oil
- 1-2 tablespoons Parmesan cheese, shredded
- 1 teaspoon fresh parsley, chopped
- Salt and ground black pepper, as required

Method:

1. Set the temperature of Ninja Max XL Air Fryer to 360 degrees F and select "Air Fry" to preheat for 5 minutes.
2. Press "Start/Pause" to begin.
3. In a small baking pan, place the sausage slices and cherry tomatoes.
4. Arrange the pan into the Air Fryer basket.
5. Slide the basket in Air Fryer and select "Air Fry" for 10 minutes.
6. Press "Start/Pause" to begin.
7. Meanwhile, in a small bowl, add the remaining ingredients and beat until well combined.
8. After 5 minutes of cooking, place the egg mixture over sausage mixture evenly.
9. Remove the pan from Air Fryer and place onto a wire rack to cool for about 5 minutes before serving.

Nutritional Information per Serving:

- Calories 489
- Total Fat 40.6 g
- Saturated Fat 10.8 g
- Cholesterol 530 mg
- Sodium 744 mg
- Total Carbs 4.8 g
- Fiber 1.1 g
- Sugar 3.4 g
- Protein 27.5 g

Date Bread

Preparation Time: 15 minutes
Cooking Time: 22 minutes
Servings: 10

Ingredients:

- 2½ cup dates, pitted and chopped
- ¼ cup butter
- 1 cup hot water
- 1½ cups flour
- ½ cup brown sugar
- 1 teaspoon baking powder
- 1 teaspoon baking soda
- ½ teaspoon salt
- 1 egg

Method:

1. In a large bowl, add the dates, butter and top with the hot water. Set aside for about 5 minutes.
2. In a separate bowl, mix together the flour, brown sugar, baking powder, baking soda, and salt.
3. In the same bowl of dates, mix well the flour mixture, and egg.
4. Set the temperature of Ninja Max XL Air Fryer to 340 degrees F and select "Air Fry" to preheat for 5 minutes. Press "Start/Pause" to begin.
5. Grease an Air Fryer non-stick pan.
6. Place the mixture into the prepared pan.
7. Arrange the pan into the Air Fryer basket.
8. Slide the basket in Air Fryer and select "Air Fry" for 22 minutes.
9. Press "Start/Pause" to begin.
10. Remove from Air Fryer and place the pan onto a wire rack for about 10-15 minutes
11. Carefully, invert the bread onto the wire rack to cool completely cool before slicing.
12. Cut the bread into desired sized slices and serve.

Nutritional Information per Serving:

- Calories 129
- Total Fat 5.4 g
- Saturated Fat 3.1 g
- Cholesterol 29 mg
- Sodium 295 mg
- Total Carbs 55.1 g
- Fiber 4.1 g
- Sugar 35.3 g
- Protein 3.6 g

Apple Muffins

Preparation Time: 15 minutes
Cooking Time: 25 minutes
Servings: 6

Ingredients:

- 1¾ cups plain flour
- 1/3 cup white sugar
- 1½ teaspoons baking powder
- ½ teaspoon ground cinnamon
- ¼ teaspoon ground ginger
- ¼ teaspoon salt
- ¾ cup milk
- 1/3 cup applesauce
- 1 cup apple, cored and chopped

Method:

1. In a large bowl, mix together the flour, sugar, baking powder, spices, and salt.
2. Add in the milk and applesauce. Beat until just combined.
3. Fold in the chopped apple.
4. Set the temperature of Ninja Max XL Air Fryer to 390 degrees F and select "Air Fry" to preheat for 5 minutes.
5. Press "Start/Pause" to begin. Grease 12 muffin molds.
6. Place the mixture into the prepared muffin molds evenly.
7. Arrange the molds into the Air Fryer basket.
8. Slide the basket in Air Fryer and select "Air Fry" for 25 minutes.
9. Press "Start/Pause" to begin.
10. Remove the muffin molds from Air Fryer and place onto a wire rack to cool for about 10 minutes.
11. Carefully, invert the muffins onto the wire rack to completely cool before serving.

Nutritional Information per Serving:

- Calories 217
- Total Fat 1.1 g
- Saturated Fat 0.4 g
- Cholesterol 3 mg
- Sodium 114 mg
- Total Carbs 47.9 g
- Fiber 2.2 g
- Sugar 17.8 g
- Protein 4.9 g

Salmon Quiche

Preparation Time: 15 minutes
Cooking Time: 20 minutes
Servings: 2

Ingredients:

- 5½ ounces salmon fillet, chopped
- Salt and ground black pepper, as required
- ½ tablespoons fresh lemon juice
- 1 egg yolk
- 3½ tablespoons chilled butter
- 2/3 cup flour
- 1 tablespoon cold water
- 2 eggs
- 3 tablespoons whipping cream
- 1 scallion, chopped

Method:

1. In a bowl, mix together the salmon, salt, black pepper and lemon juice. Set aside.
2. In another bowl, add egg yolk, butter, flour and water and mix until a dough forms.
3. Place the dough onto a floured smooth surface and roll into about 7-inch round.
4. Place the dough in a quiche pan and press firmly in the bottom and along the edges.
5. Trim the excess edges.
6. In a small bowl, add the eggs, cream, salt and black pepper and beat until well combined.
7. Place the cream mixture over crust evenly and top with the chopped salmon, followed by the scallion.
8. Set the temperature of Ninja Max XL Air Fryer to 355 degrees F and select "Air Fry" to preheat for 5 minutes.
9. Press "Start/Pause" to begin.
10. Arrange the quiche pan in Air Fryer basket.
11. Slide the basket in Air Fryer and select "Air Fry" for 20 minutes.
12. Press "Start/Pause" to begin.
13. Remove the pan from Air Fryer and place onto a wire rack to cool for about 5 minutes before serving.

Nutritional Information per Serving:

- Calories 592
- Total Fat 39 g
- Saturated Fat 20.1 g
- Cholesterol 381 mg
- Sodium 331 mg
- Total Carbs 33.8 g
- Fiber 1.4 g
- Sugar 0.8 g
- Protein 27.2 g

Banana Bread

Preparation Time: 15 minutes
Cooking Time: 35 minutes
Servings: 5

Ingredients:

- ½ cup all-purpose flour
- ¼ cup whole-wheat flour
- ¼ teaspoon baking soda
- ½ teaspoon salt
- 1 large egg
- ½ cup granulated sugar
- ¼ cup plain Greek yogurt
- ¼ cup olive oil
- ½ teaspoon pure vanilla extract
- 2 ripe bananas, peeled and mashed
- 2 tablespoons turbinado sugar

Method:

1. In a bowl, sift together the flours, baking soda, and salt.
2. In another large bowl, mix well the egg, granulated sugar, yogurt, oil, and vanilla extract.
3. Add in the bananas and beat until well combined.
4. Now, add the flour mixture and mix until just combined.
5. Set the temperature of Ninja Max XL Air Fryer to 310 degrees F and select "Air Fry" to preheat for 5 minutes.
6. Press "Start/Pause" to begin.
7. Place the mixture into a cake pan and sprinkle with the turbinado sugar.
8. Arrange the cake pan into the Air Fryer basket.
9. Slide the basket in Air Fryer and select "Air Fry" for 35 minutes.
10. Press "Start/Pause" to begin.
11. Remove from Air Fryer and place the pan onto a wire rack for about 10-15 minutes.
12. Carefully, invert the bread onto the wire rack to cool completely cool before slicing.
13. Cut the bread into desired sized slices and serve.

Nutritional Information per Serving:

- Calories 313
- Total Fat 11.7 g
- Saturated Fat 1.9 g
- Cholesterol 38 mg
- Sodium 320 mg
- Total Carbs 50 g
- Fiber 2.4 g
- Sugar 30.3 g
- Protein 4.8 g

Carrot Muffins

Preparation Time: 15 minutes
Cooking Time: 8 minutes
Servings: 6

Ingredients:

- ¼ cup whole-wheat flour
- ¼ cup all-purpose flour
- ½ teaspoon baking powder
- 1/8 teaspoon baking soda
- ½ teaspoon dried parsley, crushed
- ½ teaspoon salt
- ½ cup yogurt
- 1 teaspoon vinegar
- 1 tablespoon vegetable oil
- 3 tablespoons cottage cheese, grated
- 1 carrot, peeled and grated
- 2-4 tablespoons water (if needed)
- ¼ cup Parmesan cheese, grated
- ¼ cup walnuts, chopped

Method:

1. For muffin: in a large bowl, mix together the flours, baking powder, baking soda, parsley, and salt.
2. In another large bowl, add the yogurt and vinegar and mix well.
3. Add the remaining ingredients except for water and beat them well. (add some water if needed).
4. Make a well in the center of the yogurt mixture.
5. Slowly, add the flour mixture in the well and mix until well combined.
6. Place the mixture into the prepared muffin molds and top with the Parmesan cheese and walnuts.
7. Set the temperature of Ninja Max XL Air Fryer to 355 degrees F and select "Air Fry" to preheat for 5 minutes.
8. Press "Start/Pause" to begin. Grease 6 medium muffin molds.
9. Place the muffin molds into the Air Fryer basket.
10. Arrange the molds into the Air Fryer basket.
11. Slide the basket in Air Fryer and select "Air Fry" for 8 minutes.
12. Press "Start/Pause" to begin.
13. Remove the muffin molds from Air Fryer and place onto a wire rack to cool for about 10 minutes.
14. Carefully, invert the muffins onto the wire rack to completely cool before serving.

Nutritional Information per Serving:

- Calories 266
- Total Fat 13.5 g
- Saturated Fat 3 g
- Cholesterol 8 mg
- Sodium 654 mg
- Total Carbs 24.3 g

- Fiber 1.9 g
- Sugar 4.1 g

- Protein 12.1 g

Banana Muffins

Preparation Time: 10 minutes
Cooking Time: 15 minutes
Servings: 2

Ingredients:

- ¼ cup oats
- ¼ cup refined flour
- ½ teaspoon baking powder
- ¼ cup powdered sugar
- ¼ cup unsalted butter, softened
- ¼ cup banana, peeled and mashed
- 1 teaspoon milk
- 1 tablespoon walnuts, chopped

Method:

1. In a bowl, mix together the oats, flour and baking powder.
2. In another bowl, add the sugar and butter and beat until creamy
3. Add the banana and vanilla extract and beat until well combined.
4. Add the flour mixture and milk in banana mixture and mix until just combined.
5. Fold in the walnuts.
6. Set the temperature of Ninja Max XL Air Fryer to 320 degrees F and select "Air Fry" to preheat for 5 minutes.
7. Press "Start/Pause" to begin.
8. Grease 4 muffin molds.
9. Place the mixture into the prepared muffin molds evenly.
10. Arrange the molds into the Air Fryer basket.
11. Slide the basket in Air Fryer and select "Air Fry" for 10 minutes.
12. Press "Start/Pause" to begin.
13. Remove the muffin molds from Air Fryer and place onto a wire rack to cool for about 10 minutes.
14. Carefully, invert the muffins onto the wire rack to completely cool before serving.

Nutritional Information per Serving:

- Calories 401
- Total Fat 26.3 g
- Saturated Fat 14.9 g
- Cholesterol 61 mg
- Sodium 167 mg
- Total Carbs 39.2 g
- Fiber 2.2 g
- Sugar 17.3 g
- Protein 4.4 g

Tofu Omelet

Preparation Time: 15 minutes
Cooking Time: 29 minutes
Servings: 2

Ingredients:

- 2 teaspoons canola oil
- ¼ of onion, chopped
- 1 garlic clove, minced
- 8 ounces silken tofu, pressed and sliced
- 3½ ounces fresh mushrooms, sliced
- 1/8 teaspoon red pepper flakes, crushed
- Salt and ground black pepper, as required
- 3 eggs, beaten

Method:

1. Set the temperature of Ninja Max XL Air Fryer to 355 degrees F and select "Air Fry" to preheat for 5 minutes.
2. Press "Start/Pause" to begin.
3. In an Air Fryer pan, add the oil, onion, and garlic.
4. Slide the pan in Air Fryer and select "Air Fry" for 29 minutes.
5. Press "Start/Pause" to begin.
6. After 4 minutes of cooking, Press "Start/Pause" to pause cooking.
7. Remove the pan from Air Fryer and stir in the tofu, mushrooms, red pepper flakes, salt and black pepper.
8. Top with the beaten eggs evenly.
9. While cooking, poke the eggs after every 8 minutes.
10. Remove the pan from Air Fryer and serve hot.

Nutritional Information per Serving:

- Calories 225
- Total Fat 14.5 g
- Saturated Fat 2.9 g
- Cholesterol 246 mg
- Sodium 214 mg
- Total Carbs 6.7 g
- Fiber 1 g
- Sugar 3.4 g
- Protein 17.9 g

Cheese Omelet

Preparation Time: 5 minutes
Cooking Time: 8 minutes
Servings: 2

Ingredients:

- 4 eggs
- ¼ cup cream
- Salt and ground black pepper, as required
- ¼ cup cheddar cheese, grated

Method:

1. Set the temperature of Ninja Max XL Air Fryer to 350 degrees F and select "Air Fry" to preheat for 5 minutes.
2. Press "Start/Pause" to begin.
3. Lightly, grease a 6x3-inch pan.
4. In a bowl, add the eggs, cream, salt, and black pepper and beat until well combined.
5. Place the egg mixture into the prepared pan.
6. Arrange the pan into the Air Fryer basket.
7. Slide the basket in Air Fryer and select "Air Fry" for 8 minutes.
8. Press "Start/Pause" to begin.
9. After 4 minutes of cooking, sprinkle the cheese on the top of omelet.
10. Remove the pan from Air Fryer and with a spatula, flip the omelet.
11. Cut in 2 portions and serve hot.

Nutritional Information per Serving:

- Calories 202
- Total Fat 15.1 g
- Saturated Fat 6.8 g
- Cholesterol 348 mg
- Sodium 298 mg
- Total Carbs 1.8 g
- Fiber 0 g
- Sugar 1.4 g
- Protein 14.8 g

Veggie Frittata

Preparation Time: 15 minutes
Cooking Time: 18 minutes
Servings: 2

Ingredients:

- ¼ cup half-and-half
- 4 large eggs
- Salt and ground black pepper, as required
- 2 cups fresh spinach, chopped
- ½ cup onion, chopped
- ¼ cup tomato, chopped
- ½ cup feta cheese, crumbled

Method:

1. In a bowl, add the half-and-half, eggs, salt and black pepper and beat until well combined.
2. Add the spinach, onion, tomatoes and feta cheese and mix well.
3. Set the temperature of Ninja Max XL Air Fryer to 360 degrees F and select "Air Fry" to preheat for 5 minutes.
4. Press "Start/Pause" to begin.
5. Place the mixture into a greased round baking pan.
6. Arrange the pan into the Air Fryer basket.
7. Slide the basket in Air Fryer and select "Air Fry" for 18 minutes.
8. Press "Start/Pause" to begin.
9. Remove the pan from Air Fryer and place onto a wire rack to cool for about 5 minutes before serving.

Nutritional Information per Serving:

- Calories 304
- Total Fat 21.6 g
- Saturated Fat 10.9 g
- Cholesterol 416 mg
- Sodium 674 mg
- Total Carbs 8.3 g
- Fiber 1.6 g
- Sugar 4.3 g
- Protein 20.2 g

Chicken Omelet

Preparation Time: 10 minutes
Cooking Time: 16 minutes
Servings: 2

Ingredients:

- 1 teaspoon butter
- 1 onion, chopped
- ½ jalapeño pepper, seeded and chopped
- 3 eggs
- Salt and ground black pepper, as required
- ¼ cup cooked chicken, shredded

Method:

1. In a frying pan, melt the butter over medium heat and sauté the onion for about 4-5 minutes.
2. Add the jalapeño pepper and sauté for about 1 minute.
3. Add the chicken and stir to combine.
4. Remove from the heat and set aside.
5. Set the temperature of Ninja Max XL Air Fryer to 355 degrees F and select "Air Fry" to preheat for 5 minutes.
6. Press "Start/Pause" to begin.
7. Grease the Air Fryer pan.
8. In a bowl, add the eggs, salt, and black pepper and beat well.
9. Place the chicken mixture into the prepared pan.
10. Top with egg mixture and gently, stir to combine.
11. Slide the pan in Air Fryer and select "Air Fry" for 10 minutes.
12. Press "Start/Pause" to begin.
13. After 4 minutes of cooking, sprinkle the cheese on the top of omelet.
14. Remove the pan from Air Fryer and cut in 2 portions.
15. Serve hot.

Nutritional Information per Serving:

- Calories 161
- Total Fat 9.1 g
- Saturated Fat 3.4 g
- Cholesterol 264 mg
- Sodium 197 mg
- Total Carbs 5.9 g
- Fiber 1.3 g
- Sugar 3 g
- Protein 14.1 g

Ham Casserole

Preparation Time: 15 minutes
Cooking Time: 12 minutes
Servings: 2

Ingredients:

- 4 large eggs, divided
- Salt and ground black pepper, as required
- 2 tablespoons heavy cream
- 2 teaspoons unsalted butter, softened
- 2 ounces ham, sliced thinly
- 1/8 teaspoon smoked paprika
- 3 tablespoons Parmesan cheese, grated finely
- 2 teaspoons fresh chives, minced

Method:

1. In a bowl, add 1 egg, salt, black pepper and cream and beat until smooth.
2. In the bottom of a pie dish, spread the butter.
3. Place the ham slices over the butter and top with the egg mixture evenly.
4. Carefully, crack the remaining eggs on top and sprinkle with paprika, salt and black pepper.
5. Top with cheese and chives evenly.
6. Set the temperature of Ninja Max XL Air Fryer to 320 degrees F and select "Air Fry" to preheat for 5 minutes.
7. Press "Start/Pause" to begin.
8. Arrange the pie dish into the Air Fryer basket.
9. Slide the basket in Air Fryer and select "Air Fry" for 12 minutes.
10. Press "Start/Pause" to begin.
11. Remove the pie dish from Air Fryer and place onto a wire rack to cool for about 5 minutes before serving.

Nutritional Information per Serving:

- Calories 306
- Total Fat 23.8 g
- Saturated Fat 11.1 g
- Cholesterol 424 mg
- Sodium 747 mg
- Total Carbs 2.7 g
- Fiber 0.5 g
- Sugar 0.8 g
- Protein 20.5 g

Bacon & Egg Cups

Preparation Time: 10 minutes
Cooking Time: 23 minutes
Servings: 2

Ingredients:

- 1 bacon slice
- 2 eggs
- 2 tablespoons milk
- Ground black pepper, as required
- 1 teaspoon marinara sauce
- 1 tablespoon Parmesan cheese, grated
- 1 tablespoon fresh parsley, chopped
- 2 bread slices, toasted and buttered

Method:

1. Set the temperature of Ninja Max XL Air Fryer to 355 degrees F and select "Air Fry" to preheat for 5 minutes.
2. Press "Start/Pause" to begin.
3. Place the bacon slice in the Air Fryer basket.
4. Slide the basket in Air Fryer and select "Air Fry" for 10 minutes.
5. Press "Start/Pause" press "Start/Pause" to pause cooking and remove the bacon from Air Fryer.
6. Then cut the bacon into small pieces and divide into 2 ramekins.
7. Crack 1 egg in each ramekin over the bacon.
8. Pour the milk evenly over eggs and sprinkle with black pepper.
9. Top with marinara sauce, followed by the Parmesan cheese.
10. Place the ramekins into the Air Fryer basket.
11. Slide the basket in Air Fryer and select "Air Fry" for 8 minutes.
12. Press "Start/Pause" to begin.
13. Remove from Air Fryer and sprinkle with parsley.
14. Serve hot.

Nutritional Information per Serving:

- Calories 186
- Total Fat 11.8 g
- Saturated Fat 4.1 g
- Cholesterol 183 mg
- Sodium 519 mg
- Total Carbs 6.5 g
- Fiber 0.4 g
- Sugar 1.7 g
- Protein 13.2 g

Chapter 3: Snacks Recipes

Carrot Sticks

Preparation Time: 10 minutes
Cooking Time: 12 minutes
Servings: 2

Ingredients:

- 1 large carrot, peeled and cut into sticks
- 1 tablespoon fresh rosemary, finely chopped
- 1 tablespoon olive oil
- 2 teaspoons sugar
- ¼ teaspoon cayenne pepper
- Salt and ground black pepper, as required

Method:

1. Set the temperature of Ninja Max XL Air Fryer to 390 degrees F and select "Air Fry" to preheat for 5 minutes. Press "Start/Pause" to begin.
2. In a bowl, add all the ingredients and toss to coat well.
3. Place the carrot sticks in the Air Fryer basket in a single layer.
4. Slide the basket in Air Fryer and select "Air Fry" for 12 minutes.
5. Press "Start/Pause" to begin.
6. Remove from Air Fryer and serve.

Nutritional Information per Serving:

- Calories 96
- Total Fat 7.3 g
- Saturated Fat 1.1 g
- Cholesterol 0 mg
- Sodium 103 mg
- Total Carbs 8.7 g
- Fiber 1.7 g
- Sugar 5.8 g
- Protein 0.4 g

Banana Chips

Preparation Time: 10 minutes
Cooking Time: 10 minutes
Servings: 6

Ingredients:

- 2 raw bananas, peeled and sliced
- 2 tablespoons olive oil
- Salt and ground black pepper, as required

Method:

1. Set the temperature of Ninja Max XL Air Fryer to 355 degrees F and select "Air Fry" to preheat for 5 minutes.
2. Press "Start/Pause" to begin.
3. Drizzle the banana slices with oil evenly.
4. Arrange the banana slices in the Air Fryer basket in a single layer.
5. Slide the basket in Air Fryer and select "Air Fry" for 10 minutes.
6. Press "Start/Pause" to begin.
7. Remove from Air Fryer and transfer the banana chips into a bowl.
8. Sprinkle with salt and black pepper and serve.

Nutritional Information per Serving:

- Calories 75
- Total Fat 4.8 g
- Saturated Fat 0.7 g
- Cholesterol 0 mg
- Sodium 28 mg
- Total Carbs 9 g
- Fiber 1 g
- Sugar 4.8 g
- Protein 0.4 g

Roasted Cashews

Preparation Time: 10 minutes
Cooking Time: 4 minutes
Servings: 8

Ingredients:

- 2 cups raw cashew nuts
- 1 teaspoon butter, melted
- Salt and ground black pepper, as required

Method:

1. Set the temperature of Ninja Max XL Air Fryer to 355 degrees F and select "Air Fry" to preheat for 5 minutes.
2. Press "Start/Pause" to begin.
3. In a bowl, mix together all the ingredients.
4. Place the cashews nuts in the Air Fryer basket in a single layer.
5. Slide the basket in Air Fryer and select "Air Fry" for 4 minutes.
6. Press "Start/Pause" to begin.
7. While cooking, shake the basket once halfway through.
8. Remove from Air Fryer and serve.

Nutritional Information per Serving:

- Calories 201
- Total Fat 16.4 g
- Saturated Fat 3.4 g
- Cholesterol 1 mg
- Sodium 28 mg
- Total Carbs 11.2 g
- Fiber 1 g
- Sugar 1.7 g
- Protein 5.3 g

Buttered Corn

Preparation Time: 5 minutes
Cooking Time: 20 minutes
Servings: 2

Ingredients:

- 2 corn on the cob
- Salt and ground black pepper, as required
- 2 tablespoons butter, softened and divided

Method:

1. Set the temperature of Ninja Max XL Air Fryer to 320 degrees F and select "Air Fry" to preheat for 5 minutes.
2. Press "Start/Pause" to begin.
3. Sprinkle the cobs evenly with salt and black pepper.
4. Then, rub with 1 tablespoon of butter.
5. With 1 piece of foil, wrap each cob and place in the Air Fryer basket.
6. Slide the basket in Air Fryer and select "Air Fry" for 20 minutes.
7. Press "Start/Pause" to begin.
8. Remove from Air Fryer and transfer the cobs onto a plate.
9. Drizzle with the remaining butter and serve.

Nutritional Information per Serving:

- Calories 265
- Total Fat 12.8 g
- Saturated Fat 7.5 g
- Cholesterol 31 mg
- Sodium 166 mg
- Total Carbs 39.1 g
- Fiber 4.9 g
- Sugar 6.3 g
- Protein 5.6 g

Kale Chips

Preparation Time: 10 minutes
Cooking Time: 3 minutes
Servings: 4

Ingredients:

- 1 head fresh kale, stems and ribs removed and cut into 1½ inch pieces
- 1 tablespoon olive oil
- 1 teaspoon soy sauce
- 1/8 teaspoon cayenne pepper
- Pinch of freshly ground black pepper

Method:

1. Set the temperature of Ninja Max XL Air Fryer to 390 degrees F and select "Air Fry" to preheat for 5 minutes.
2. Press "Start/Pause" to begin.
3. In a large bowl, add all the ingredients and mix well.
4. Place the kale pieces in the Air Fryer basket in a single layer.
5. Slide the basket in Air Fryer and select "Air Fry" for 3 minutes.
6. Press "Start/Pause" to begin.
7. While cooking, toss the kale pieces once halfway through.
8. Remove from Air Fryer and set aside for 5minutes before serving.

Nutritional Information per Serving:

- Calories 55
- Total Fat 3.5 g
- Saturated Fat 0.5 g
- Cholesterol 0 mg
- Sodium 96 mg
- Total Carbs 5.3 g
- Fiber 0.8 g
- Sugar 0 g
- Protein 1.6 g

Cauliflower Poppers

Preparation Time: 10 minutes
Cooking Time: 16 minutes
Servings: 6

Ingredients:

- 1 large head cauliflower, cut into bite-sized florets
- 2 tablespoons olive oil
- Salt and ground black pepper, as required

Method:

1. Drizzle the cauliflower florets with oil and sprinkle with salt and black pepper.
2. Set the temperature of Ninja Max XL Air Fryer to 390 degrees F and select "Air Fry" to preheat for 5 minutes.
3. Press "Start/Pause" to begin.
4. Place the cauliflower florets in a greased Air Fryer basket in a single layer in 2 batches.
5. Slide the basket in Air Fryer and select "Air Fry" for 8 minutes.
6. Press "Start/Pause" to begin.
7. While cooking, shake the basket once halfway through.
8. Remove from Air Fryer and serve hot.

Nutritional Information per Serving:

- Calories 51
- Total Fat 4.7 g
- Saturated Fat 0.7 g
- Cholesterol 0 mg
- Sodium 40 mg
- Total Carbs 2.3 g
- Fiber 1.1 g
- Sugar 1.1 g
- Protein 0.9 g

Roasted Peanuts

Preparation Time: 5 minutes
Cooking Time: 14 minutes
Servings: 5

Ingredients:

- 1¼ cups raw peanuts
- ½ tablespoon olive oil
- Salt, as required

Method:

1. Set the temperature of Ninja Max XL Air Fryer to 355 degrees F and select "Air Fry" to preheat for 5 minutes.
2. Press "Start/Pause" to begin.
3. Place the peanuts in the Air Fryer basket in a single layer.
4. Slide the basket in Air Fryer and select "Air Fry" for 15 minutes.
5. Press "Start/Pause" to begin.
6. After 9 minutes of cooking, Press "Start/Pause" to pause cooking.
7. Remove the basket from Air Fryer and transfer the peanuts into a large bowl.
8. Add the oil and salt and toss to coat well.
9. Return the peanuts into the Air Fryer basket.
10. Slide the basket in Air Fryer and press "Start/Pause" to resume cooking.
11. Remove from Air Fryer and serve.

Nutritional Information per Serving:

- Calories 219
- Total Fat 19.4 g
- Saturated Fat 2.7 g
- Cholesterol 0 mg
- Sodium 38 mg
- Total Carbs 5.9 g
- Fiber 3.1 g
- Sugar 1.5 g
- Protein 9.4 g

Spicy Chickpeas

Preparation Time: 5 minutes
Cooking Time: 10 minutes
Servings: 2

Ingredients:

- ½ (15-ounce) can chickpeas, rinsed and drained
- ½ tablespoon olive oil
- ¼ teaspoon ground cumin
- ¼ teaspoon cayenne pepper
- ¼ teaspoon smoked paprika
- Salt, as required

Method:

1. Set the temperature of Ninja Max XL Air Fryer to 390 degrees F and select "Air Fry" to preheat for 5 minutes.
2. Press "Start/Pause" to begin.
3. In a bowl, add all the ingredients and toss to coat well.
4. Place the chickpeas in the Air Fryer basket in a single layer.
5. Slide the basket in Air Fryer and select "Air Fry" for 10 minutes.
6. Press "Start/Pause" to begin.
7. Remove from Air Fryer and serve.

Nutritional Information per Serving:

- Calories 207
- Total Fat 6.4 g
- Saturated Fat 0.8 g
- Cholesterol 0 mg
- Sodium 86 mg
- Total Carbs 29.5 g
- Fiber 8.3 g
- Sugar 5.2 g
- Protein 9.5 g

French Fries

Preparation Time: 5 minutes
Cooking Time: 23 minutes
Servings: 8

Ingredients:

- 1 pound frozen French fries
- Salt, as required

Method:

1. Set the temperature of Ninja Max XL Air Fryer to 350 degrees F and select "Air Fry" to preheat for 3 minutes.
2. Press "Start/Pause" to begin.
3. Place the crisper plate in the basket and insert in the Air Fryer while heating.
4. Place the fries in over the crisper plate.
5. Slide the basket in Air Fryer and select "Air Fry" for 23 minutes.
6. Press "Start/Pause" to begin.
7. After 10 minutes, press "Start/Pause" to pause cooking.
8. Remove basket from Air Fryer and toss the fries.
9. Again, slide the basket in Air Fryer and press "Start/Pause" to resume cooking.
10. Repeat the process of tossing after 20 minutes of cooking.
11. Remove basket from Air Fryer and transfer the fries into a large bowl.
12. Sprinkle with salt and toss to coat.
13. Serve hot.

Nutritional Information per Serving:

- Calories 131
- Total Fat 5.7 g
- Saturated Fat 1 g
- Cholesterol 0 mg
- Sodium 152 mg
- Total Carbs 18 g
- Fiber 2 g
- Sugar 0.5 g
- Protein 2 g

Tortilla Chips

Preparation Time: 10 minutes
Cooking Time: 3 minutes
Servings: 3

Ingredients:

- 4 corn tortillas, cut into triangles
- ½ tablespoon olive oil
- Salt, as required

Method:

1. Set the temperature of Ninja Max XL Air Fryer to 390 degrees F and select "Air Fry" to preheat for 5 minutes.
2. Press "Start/Pause" to begin.
3. Coat the tortilla chips with oil and sprinkle with salt.
4. Place the tortilla triangles in the Air Fryer basket in a single layer.
5. Slide the basket in Air Fryer and select "Air Fry" for 3 minutes.
6. Press "Start/Pause" to begin.
7. Remove from Air Fryer and serve.

Nutritional Information per Serving:

- Calories 90
- Total Fat 3.2 g
- Saturated Fat 0.5 g
- Cholesterol 0 mg
- Sodium 65 mg
- Total Carbs 14.3 g
- Fiber 2 g
- Sugar 0.3 g
- Protein 1.8 g

Buttermilk Biscuits

Preparation Time: 15 minutes
Cooking Time: 8 minutes
Servings: 6

Ingredients:

- ½ cup cake flour
- 1¼ cups all-purpose flour
- ¼ teaspoon baking soda
- ½ teaspoon baking powder
- 1 teaspoon granulated sugar
- Salt, as required
- ¼ cup cold unsalted butter, cut into cubes
- ¾ cup buttermilk
- 2 tablespoons butter, melted

Method:

1. In a large bowl, sift together the flours, baking soda, baking powder, sugar, and salt.
2. With a pastry cutter, cut in ¼ cup of butter until coarse crumb forms.
3. Slowly, add in the buttermilk and mix until a smooth dough forms.
4. Place the dough onto a floured surface and with your hands, press it into ½ inch thickness.
5. With a 1¾-inch round cookie cutter, cut the biscuits.
6. Set the temperature of Ninja Max XL Air Fryer to 400 degrees F and select "Air Fry" to preheat for 5 minutes.
7. Press "Start/Pause" to begin.
8. Place the biscuits in a lightly greased pie pan in a single layer and coat with melted butter.
9. Place the pie pan in the Air Fryer basket.
10. Slide the basket in Air Fryer and select "Air Fry" for 8 minutes.
11. Press "Start/Pause" to begin.
12. Remove from Air Fryer and serve warm.

Nutritional Information per Serving:

- Calories 266
- Total Fat 12.2 g
- Saturated Fat 7.5 g
- Cholesterol 32 mg
- Sodium 194 mg
- Total Carbs 33.6 g
- Fiber 1.3 g
- Sugar 2.2 g
- Protein 6 g

Zucchini Fries

Preparation Time: 10 minutes
Cooking Time: 10 minutes
Servings: 3

Ingredients:

- ½ pound zucchini, sliced into 2½-inch sticks
- Salt, as required
- 1 tablespoon olive oil
- 1/3 cup panko breadcrumbs

Method:

1. In a colander, add the zucchini and sprinkle with salt. Set aside for about 10 minutes.
2. Set the temperature of Ninja Max XL Air Fryer to 390 degrees F and select "Air Fry" to preheat for 5 minutes.
3. Press "Start/Pause" to begin.
4. Gently pat dry the zucchini sticks with the paper towels and coat with oil.
5. In a shallow dish, add the breadcrumbs.
6. Coat the zucchini sticks with breadcrumbs evenly.
7. Place the zucchini sticks in the Air Fryer basket in a single layer.
8. Slide the basket in Air Fryer and set the temperature to 425 degrees F for 10 minutes.
9. Press "Start/Pause" to begin.
10. Remove basket from Air Fryer and serve.

Nutritional Information per Serving:

- Calories 95
- Total Fat 5.6 g
- Saturated Fat 1 g
- Cholesterol 0 mg
- Sodium 58 mg
- Total Carbs 4.4 g
- Fiber 0.9 g
- Sugar 1.3 g
- Protein 1.2 g

Onion Rings

Preparation Time: 15 minutes
Cooking Time: 10 minutes
Servings: 4

Ingredients:

- 1 large onion, cut into ¼ inch slices
- 1¼ cups all-purpose flour
- 1 teaspoon baking powder
- Salt, as required
- 1 cup milk
- 1 egg
- ¾ cup dry breadcrumbs

Method:

1. Separate the onion slices into rings.
2. In a shallow dish, mix together the flour, baking powder, and salt.
3. In a second dish, add the milk and egg and beat well.
4. In a third dish, put the breadcrumbs.
5. Coat each onion ring with flour mixture, then dip into egg mixture and finally, coat with the breadcrumbs.
6. Set the temperature of Ninja Max XL Air Fryer to 360 degrees F and select "Air Fry" to preheat for 5 minutes.
7. Press "Start/Pause" to begin.
8. Place the onion rings in the Air Fryer basket in a single layer.
9. Slide the basket in Air Fryer and select "Air Fry" for 10 minutes.
10. Press "Start/Pause" to begin.
11. Remove from Air Fryer and serve hot.

Nutritional Information per Serving:

- Calories 285
- Total Fat 3.8 g
- Saturated Fat 1.4 g
- Cholesterol 46 mg
- Sodium 235 mg
- Total Carbs 51.6 g
- Fiber 2.8 g
- Sugar 5.8 g
- Protein 10.5 g

Coconut Cookies

Preparation Time: 15 minutes
Cooking Time: 12 minutes
Servings: 8

Ingredients:

- 2¼ ounces caster sugar
- 3½ ounces butter
- 1 small egg
- 1 teaspoon vanilla extract
- 5 ounces self-rising flour
- 1¼ ounces white chocolate, chopped
- 3 tablespoons desiccated coconut

Method:

1. In a large bowl, add the sugar, and butter and beat until fluffy and light.
2. Add the egg, and vanilla extract and beat until well combined
3. Now, add the flour, and chocolate and mix well.
4. In a shallow bowl, place the coconut.
5. With your hands, make small balls from the mixture and roll evenly into the coconut.
6. Place the balls onto an ungreased baking sheet about 1- inch apart and gently, press each ball.
7. Set the temperature of Ninja Max XL Air Fryer to 355 degrees F and select "Air Fry" to preheat for 5 minutes.
8. Press "Start/Pause" to begin.
9. Place the baking sheet into the Air Fryer basket.
10. Slide the basket in Air Fryer and select "Air Fry" for 8 minutes.
11. Press "Start/Pause" to begin.
12. Remove from Air Fryer and place the baking sheet onto a wire rack to cool for about 5 minutes.
13. Now, invert the cookies onto the wire rack to cool completely before serving.

Nutritional Information per Serving:

- Calories 222
- Total Fat 12.7 g
- Saturated Fat 8 g
- Cholesterol 45 mg
- Sodium 83 mg
- Total Carbs 24.5 g
- Fiber 0.7 g
- Sugar 10.9 g
- Protein 2.8 g

Crispy Bread Slices

Preparation Time: 10 minutes
Cooking Time: 5 minutes
Servings: 4

Ingredients:

- ¼ cup chickpea flour
- 3 tablespoons onion, finely chopped
- 2 teaspoons green chili, seeded and finely chopped
- ½ teaspoon red chili powder
- ¼ teaspoon ground turmeric
- ¼ teaspoon ground cumin
- Salt, as required
- Water, as needed
- 4 bread slices

Method:

1. Set the temperature of Ninja Max XL Air Fryer to 390 degrees F and select "Air Fry" to preheat for 3 minutes.
2. Press "Start/Pause" to begin.
3. Add all the ingredients except bread slices in a large bowl and mix until a thick mixture forms.
4. With a spoon, spread the mixture over both sides of each bread slice.
5. Arrange the bread slices into a lightly greased Air Fryer basket.
6. Slide the basket in Air Fryer and select "Air Fry" for 5 minutes.
7. Press "Start/Pause" to begin.
8. Flip the bread slices once halfway through.
9. Remove from Air Fryer and serve warm.

Nutritional Information per Serving:

- Calories 74
- Total Fat 1.2 g
- Saturated Fat 0.2 g
- Cholesterol 0 mg
- Sodium 107 mg
- Total Carbs 13.2 g
- Fiber 2.7 g
- Sugar 2.1 g
- Protein 3.3 g

Chapter 4: Appetizer Recipes

Mozzarella Sticks

Preparation Time: 15 minutes
Cooking Time: 12 minutes
Servings: 4

Ingredients:

- ¼ cup white flour
- 1 egg
- 1½ tablespoons nonfat milk
- ½ cup plain breadcrumbs
- ½ pound Mozzarella cheese block cut into 3x½-inch sticks

Method:

1. In a shallow dish, place the flour.
2. In a second dish, mix together the eggs and milk.
3. In a third dish, put the breadcrumbs.
4. Coat the Mozzarella sticks with flour, then dip into egg mixture and finally, coat with the breadcrumbs.
5. Arrange the Mozzarella sticks onto a baking sheet and freeze for about 1-2 hours.
6. Set the temperature of Ninja Max XL Air Fryer to 440 degrees F and select "Air Fry" to preheat for 5 minutes.
7. Press "Start/Pause" to begin.
8. Arrange the Mozzarella sticks in the Air Fryer basket in a single layer.
9. Slide the basket in Air Fryer and select "Air Fry" for 12 minutes.
10. Press "Start/Pause" to begin.
11. Remove from Air Fryer and serve warm.

Nutritional Information per Serving:

- Calories 110
- Total Fat 2.5 g
- Saturated Fat 0.9 g
- Cholesterol 43 mg
- Sodium 139 mg
- Total Carbs 16.2 g
- Fiber 0.8 g
- Sugar 1.2 g
- Protein 5.2 g

Mixed Veggie Bites

Preparation Time: 15 minutes
Cooking Time: 10 minutes
Servings: 10

Ingredients:

- 1½ pounds fresh spinach, blanched, drained and chopped
- ½ of onion, chopped
- 1 carrot, peeled and chopped
- 1 garlic clove, minced
- 2 American cheese slices, cut into tiny pieces
- 2 bread slices, toasted and processed into breadcrumbs
- 1 tablespoon cornflour
- 1 teaspoon red chili flakes
- Salt, as required

Method:

1. In a bowl, add all the ingredients except for breadcrumbs in a bowl and mix until well combined.
2. Add the breadcrumbs and gently stir to combine.
3. Make 20 equal-sized balls from the mixture.
4. Set the temperature of Ninja Max XL Air Fryer to 355 degrees F and select "Air Fry" to preheat for 5 minutes.
5. Press "Start/Pause" to begin.
6. Place the balls in the Air Fryer basket in a single layer.
7. Slide the basket in Air Fryer and set the temperature to 200 degrees F for 10 minutes.
8. Press "Start/Pause" to begin.
9. Remove from Air Fryer and serve hot.

Nutritional Information per Serving:

- Calories 47
- Total Fat 1.8 g
- Saturated Fat 0.9 g
- Cholesterol 5 mg
- Sodium 158 mg
- Total Carbs 5.6 g
- Fiber 1.9 g
- Sugar 1.3 g
- Protein 3.3 g

Rice Bites

Preparation Time: 15 minutes
Cooking Time: 20 minutes
Servings: 4

Ingredients:

- 3 cups cooked risotto
- 1/3 cup Parmesan cheese, grated
- 1 egg, beaten
- 3 ounces mozzarella cheese, cubed
- ¾ cup breadcrumbs

Method:

1. In a bowl, mix together the risotto, Parmesan cheese, and egg.
2. Make 20 equal-sized balls from the mixture.
3. Insert a mozzarella cube in the center of each ball.
4. With your fingers, smooth the risotto mixture to cover the mozzarella.
5. In a shallow dish, add the breadcrumbs.
6. Coat the balls with breadcrumbs.
7. Set the temperature of Ninja Max XL Air Fryer to 390 degrees F and select "Air Fry" to preheat for 5 minutes.
8. Press "Start/Pause" to begin.
9. Arrange the balls in the Air Fryer basket in a single layer in 2 batches.
10. Slide the basket in Air Fryer and set the temperature of Ninja Max XL Air Fryer to 200 degrees F for 10 minutes.
11. Press "Start/Pause" to begin.
12. Remove from Air Fryer and serve hot.

Nutritional Information per Serving:

- Calories 241
- Total Fat 5.2 g
- Saturated Fat 2.5 g
- Cholesterol 38 mg
- Sodium 232 mg
- Total Carbs 36.9 g
- Fiber 0.9 g
- Sugar 0.9 g
- Protein 10.7 g

Broccoli Bites

Preparation Time: 15 minutes
Cooking Time: 12 minutes
Servings: 10

Ingredients:

- 2 cups broccoli florets
- 2 eggs, beaten
- 1¼ cups cheddar cheese, grated
- ¼ cup Parmesan cheese, grated
- 1¼ cups panko breadcrumbs
- Salt and ground black pepper, as required

Method:

1. In a food processor, add the broccoli and pulse until finely crumbled.
2. In a large bowl, add the broccoli with the remaining ingredients and mix well.
3. Make small equal-sized balls from the mixture.
4. Arrange the balls in a baking sheet and refrigerate for at least 30 minutes.
5. Set the temperature of Ninja Max XL Air Fryer to 350 degrees F and select "Air Fry" to preheat for 5 minutes.
6. Press "Start/Pause" to begin.
7. Arrange the balls in the Air Fryer basket.
8. Slide the basket in Air Fryer and select "Air Fry" for 12 minutes.
9. Press "Start/Pause" to begin.
10. Remove from Air Fryer and serve warm.

Nutritional Information per Serving:

- Calories 122
- Total Fat 6.8 g
- Saturated Fat 3.8 g
- Cholesterol 49 mg
- Sodium 139 mg
- Total Carbs 3.1 g
- Fiber 0.5 g
- Sugar 0.5 g
- Protein 6.2 g

Buffalo Chicken Wings

Preparation Time: 15 minutes
Cooking Time: 22 minutes
Servings: 4

Ingredients:

- 2 pounds chicken wings, cut into drumettes and flats
- 1 teaspoon chicken seasoning
- 1 teaspoon garlic powder
- Ground black pepper, as required
- 1 tablespoon olive oil
- ¼ cup red hot sauce
- 2 tablespoons low-sodium soy sauce

Method:

1. Set the temperature of Ninja Max XL Air Fryer to 400 degrees F and select "Air Fry" to preheat for 5 minutes.
2. Press "Start/Pause" to begin.
3. Grease the Air Fryer basket.
4. Sprinkle each chicken wing with chicken seasoning, garlic powder, and black pepper.
5. Arrange chicken wings into the prepared Air Fryer basket in a single layer and drizzle with oil.
6. Slide the basket in Air Fryer and select "Air Fry" for 22 minutes.
7. Press "Start/Pause" to begin.
8. While cooking, shake the basket once after 5 minutes.
9. After 10 minutes, press "Start/Pause" to pause cooking.
10. Remove basket from Air Fryer and transfer the chicken wings into a bowl.
11. Drizzle with the red hot sauce, oil, and soy sauce and toss to coat well.
12. Place chicken wings into the Air Fryer basket in a single layer.
13. Slide the basket in Air Fryer and press "Start/Pause" to resume cooking.
14. Remove from Air Fryer and transfer the chicken wings onto a serving platter.
15. Serve hot.

Nutritional Information per Serving:

- Calories 467
- Total Fat 20.4 g
- Saturated Fat 5.1 g
- Cholesterol 202 mg
- Sodium 1029 mg
- Total Carbs 1.3 g
- Fiber 0.1 g
- Sugar 0.9 g
- Protein 3 g

Potato Croquettes

Preparation Time: 15 minutes
Cooking Time: 23 minutes
Servings: 4

Ingredients:

- 2 medium Russet potatoes, peeled and cubed
- 2 tablespoons all-purpose flour
- ½ cup Parmesan cheese, grated
- 1 egg yolk
- 2 tablespoons chives, minced
- Pinch of ground nutmeg
- Salt and ground black pepper, as required
- 2 eggs
- ½ cup breadcrumbs
- 2 tablespoons vegetable oil

Method:

1. In a pan of boiling water, add potatoes and cook for about 15 minutes.
2. Drain the potatoes well and transfer into a large bowl.
3. With a potato masher, mash the potatoes and set aside to cool completely.
4. In the same bowl of mashed potatoes, add in the flour, Parmesan cheese, egg yolk, chives, nutmeg, salt, and black pepper and mix until well combined.
5. Make small equal-sized balls from the mixture.
6. Now, roll each ball into a cylinder shape.
7. In a shallow dish, crack the eggs and beat well.
8. In another dish, mix together the breadcrumbs and oil.
9. Dip the croquettes in egg mixture and then coat with the breadcrumbs mixture.
10. Set the temperature of Ninja Max XL Air Fryer to 390 degrees F and select "Air Fry" to preheat for 5 minutes.
11. Press "Start/Pause" to begin.
12. Place the croquettes in the Air Fryer basket in a single layer.
13. Slide the basket in Air Fryer and select "Air Fry" for 8 minutes.
14. Press "Start/Pause" to begin.
15. Remove from Air Fryer and serve warm.

Nutritional Information per Serving:

- Calories 283
- Total Fat 13.4 g
- Saturated Fat 3.8 g
- Cholesterol 142 mg
- Sodium 263 mg
- Total Carbs 29.9 g
- Fiber 3.3 g
- Sugar 2.3 g
- Protein 11.5 g

Bread Rolls

Preparation Time: 20 minutes
Cooking Time: 33 minutes
Servings: 8

Ingredients:

- 5 large potatoes, peeled
- 2 tablespoons vegetable oil, divided
- 2 small onions, finely chopped
- 2 green chilies, seeded and chopped
- 2 curry leaves
- ½ teaspoon ground turmeric
- Salt, as required
- 8 bread slices, trimmed

Method:

1. In a pan of the boiling water, add the potatoes and cook for about 15-20 minutes.
2. Drain the potatoes well and with a potato masher, mash the potatoes.
3. In a skillet, heat 1 teaspoon of oil over a medium heat and sauté the onion for about 4-5 minutes.
4. Add the green chilies, curry leaves, and turmeric and sauté for about 1 minute.
5. Add in the mashed potatoes, and salt and mix well.
6. Remove from the heat and set aside to cool completely.
7. Make 8 equal-sized oval-shaped patties from the mixture.
8. Wet the bread slices completely with water.
9. With your hands, press each bread slices to remove the excess water.
10. Place 1 bread slice in your palm and place 1 patty in the center.
11. Roll the bread slice in a spindle shape and seal the edges to secure the filling.
12. Coat the roll with some oil.
13. Repeat with the remaining slices, filling and oil.
14. Set the temperature of Ninja Max XL Air Fryer to 390 degrees F and select "Air Fry" to preheat for 5 minutes.
15. Press "Start/Pause" to begin.
16. Grease the Air Fryer basket.
17. Place the rolls into the prepared basket in a single layer.
18. Slide the basket in Air Fryer and select "Air Fry" for 13 minutes.
19. Press "Start/Pause" to begin.
20. Remove from Air Fryer and serve warm.

Nutritional Information per Serving:

- Calories 221
- Total Fat 4 g
- Saturated Fat 0.8 g
- Cholesterol 0 mg
- Sodium 95 mg
- Total Carbs 42.6 g

- Fiber 6.2 g
- Sugar 3.8 g
- Protein 4.8 g

Bacon-Wrapped Scallops

Preparation Time: 15 minutes
Cooking Time: 12 minutes
Servings: 10

Ingredients:

- 5 center-cut bacon slices, cut each in 4 pieces
- 20 sea scallops, cleaned and patted very dry
- 1 teaspoon lemon pepper seasoning
- ½ teaspoon paprika
- Olive oil cooking spray
- Salt and ground black pepper, as required

Method:

1. With a piece of bacon, wrap each scallop and secure each with a toothpick.
2. Sprinkle each scallop with lemon pepper seasoning and paprika
3. Set the temperature of Ninja Max XL Air Fryer to 400 degrees F and select "Air Fry" to preheat for 5 minutes.
4. Press "Start/Pause" to begin.
5. Grease the Air Fryer basket.
6. Arrange scallops into the prepared Air Fryer basket in a single layer in 2 batches.
7. Spray the scallops with cooking spray and sprinkle with salt and black pepper.
8. Slide the basket in Air Fryer and select "Air Fry" for 6 minutes.
9. Press "Start/Pause" to begin.
10. While cooking, flip the scallops once halfway through.
11. Remove from Air Fryer and transfer the scallops onto a paper towel-lined plate.
12. Serve hot.

Nutritional Information per Serving:

- Calories 132
- Total Fat 6.5 g
- Saturated Fat 2 g
- Cholesterol 36 mg
- Sodium 447 mg
- Total Carbs 1.8 g
- Fiber 0.1 g
- Sugar 0 g
- Protein 15.5 g

Chicken Taquitos

Preparation Time: 20 minutes
Cooking Time: 15 minutes
Servings: 12

Ingredients:

- 8 ounces low-fat cream cheese, softened
- 2 tablespoons buffalo sauce
- 2 cups cooked chicken, shredded
- 12 small corn tortillas

Method:

1. In a bowl, add cream cheese and buffalo sauce and mix until smooth.
2. Add the shredded chicken and mix well.
3. Arrange the corn tortillas onto a clean, smooth surface.
4. Spread about 2-3 tablespoons of the chicken mixture onto center of each tortilla in a thin layer.
5. Roll each tortilla up tightly around the chicken mixture.
6. Set the temperature of Ninja Max XL Air Fryer to 400 degrees F and select "Air Fry" to preheat for 5 minutes.
7. Press "Start/Pause" to begin.
8. Grease the Air Fryer basket.
9. Arrange the taquitos into prepared cooking basket in a single layer.
10. Slide the basket in Air Fryer and select "Air Fry" for 15 minutes.
11. Press "Start/Pause" to begin.
12. Remove from Air Fryer and serve warm.

Nutritional Information per Serving:

- Calories 167
- Total Fat 9.2 g
- Saturated Fat 4.5 g
- Cholesterol 39 mg
- Sodium 81 mg
- Total Carbs 11.9 g
- Fiber 1.5 g
- Sugar 0.4 g
- Protein 9.6 g

Spring Rolls

Preparation Time: 20 minutes
Cooking Time: 15 minutes
Servings: 6

Ingredients:

- 2 tablespoons vegetable oil, divided
- 1¾ ounces fresh mushrooms, sliced
- 1 ounce canned water chestnuts, sliced
- 1 teaspoon fresh ginger, finely grated
- 1 ounce bean sprouts
- 1 small carrot, peeled and cut into matchsticks
- 2 scallions (green part), chopped
- 1 tablespoon soy sauce
- 1 teaspoon Chinese five-spice powder
- 3½ ounces cooked shrimp
- 12 spring roll wrappers
- 1 egg, beaten

Method:

1. In a skillet, heat 1 tablespoon of oil over medium heat and sauté the mushrooms, water chestnuts, and ginger for about 2-3 minutes.
2. Add the beans sprouts, carrot, scallion, soy sauce, and five-spice powder. Sauté for about 1 minute.
3. Stir in the shrimp and remove from heat. Set aside to cool.
4. Divide the shrimp mixture between spring rolls evenly.
5. Roll the wrappers around the filling and seal with beaten egg.
6. Coat each roll with the remaining oil.
7. Set the temperature of Ninja Max XL Air Fryer to 390 degrees F and select "Air Fry" to preheat for 5 minutes.
8. Press "Start/Pause" to begin.
9. Grease the Air Fryer basket.
10. Place rolls into the prepared Air Fryer basket in a single layer in 2 batches.
11. Slide the basket in Air Fryer and select "Air Fry" for 5 minutes.
12. Press "Start/Pause" to begin.
13. Remove from Air Fryer and serve warm.

Nutritional Information per Serving:

- Calories 274
- Total Fat 6.6 g
- Saturated Fat 1.4 g
- Cholesterol 68 mg
- Sodium 575 mg
- Total Carbs 41.1 g
- Fiber 1.6 g
- Sugar 0.8 g
- Protein 11.9 g

Crispy Prawns

Preparation Time: 15 minutes
Cooking Time: 8 minutes
Servings: 5

Ingredients:

- 1 egg
- ½ pound nacho chips, crushed
- 15 prawns, peeled and deveined

Method:

1. In a shallow dish, crack the egg, and beat well.
2. In another dish, place the crushed nacho chips.
3. Dip the prawn into beaten egg and then, coat with the nacho chips.
4. Set the temperature of Ninja Max XL Air Fryer to 355 degrees F and select "Air Fry" to preheat for 5 minutes. Press "Start/Pause" to begin.
5. Place the prawns in the Air Fryer basket in a single layer.
6. Slide the basket in Air Fryer and select "Air Fry" for 8 minutes.
7. Press "Start/Pause" to begin.
8. Remove from Air Fryer and serve hot.

Nutritional Information per Serving:

- Calories 324
- Total Fat 13.8 g
- Saturated Fat 2.4 g
- Cholesterol 173 mg
- Sodium 452 mg
- Total Carbs 29.1 g
- Fiber 2.1 g
- Sugar 1.8 g
- Protein 19.8 g

BBQ Chicken Wings

Preparation Time: 10 minutes
Cooking Time: 30 minutes
Servings: 4

Ingredients:

- 2 pounds chicken wings, cut into drumettes and flats
- ½ cup BBQ sauce

Method:

1. Set the temperature of Ninja Max XL Air Fryer to 380 degrees F and select "Air Fry" to preheat for 5 minutes.
2. Press "Start/Pause" to begin.
3. Grease the Air Fryer basket.
4. Arrange chicken wings into the prepared Air Fryer basket in a single layer.
5. Slide the basket in Air Fryer and select "Air Fry" for 24 minutes.
6. Press "Start/Pause" to begin.
7. While cooking, flip the wings once halfway through.
8. Now, set the temperature of Ninja Max XL Air Fryer to 400 degrees F for 6 minutes.
9. Remove from Air Fryer and transfer the chicken wings into a bowl.
10. Drizzle with the BBQ sauce and toss to coat well.
11. Serve immediately.

Nutritional Information per Serving:

- Calories 478
- Total Fat 16.9 g
- Saturated Fat 4.6 g
- Cholesterol 202 mg
- Sodium 545 mg
- Total Carbs 11.3 g
- Fiber 0.2 g
- Sugar 8.1 g
- Protein 65.6 g

Bacon-Wrapped Shrimp

Preparation Time: 15 minutes
Cooking Time: 7 minutes
Servings: 6

Ingredients:

- 1 pound bacon, thinly sliced
- 1 pound shrimp, peeled and deveined

Method:

1. Wrap each shrimp with one bacon slice.
2. Arrange the shrimp in a baking dish and refrigerate for about 20 minutes.
3. Set the temperature of Ninja Max XL Air Fryer to 390 degrees F and select "Air Fry" to preheat for 5 minutes.
4. Press "Start/Pause" to begin.
5. Place the shrimp in the Air Fryer basket in a single layer.
6. Slide the basket in Air Fryer and select "Air Fry" for 8 minutes.
7. Press "Start/Pause" to begin.
8. Remove from Air Fryer and serve hot.

Nutritional Information per Serving:

- Calories 499
- Total Fat 32.9 g
- Saturated Fat 10.8 g
- Cholesterol 242 mg
- Sodium 1900 mg
- Total Carbs 2.2 g
- Fiber 0 g
- Sugar 0 g
- Protein 45.2 g

Spinach Rolls

Preparation Time: 20 minutes
Cooking Time: 4 minutes
Servings: 6

Ingredients:

- 1 (16-ounce) package frozen spinach, thawed
- 1 red onion, chopped
- 1 cup fresh parsley, chopped
- 1 cup fresh mint leaves, chopped
- 1 egg
- 1 cup feta cheese, crumbled
- ½ cup Romano cheese, grated
- ¼ teaspoon ground cardamom
- Salt and ground black pepper, as required
- 1 package frozen filo dough, thawed
- 2 tablespoons olive oil

Method:

1. In a food processor, add all the ingredients except for filo dough and oil and pulse until smooth.
2. Place 1filo sheet on the cutting board and cut into three rectangular strips.
3. Brush each strip with the oil.
4. Add about1 teaspoon of spinach mixture along with the short side of a strip.
5. Roll the dough to secure the filling.
6. Repeat with the remaining filo sheets and spinach mixture.
7. Set the temperature of Ninja Max XL Air Fryer to 355 degrees F and select "Air Fry" to preheat for 5 minutes.
8. Press "Start/Pause" to begin.
9. Grease the Air Fryer basket.
10. Arrange the rolls into the prepared basket in a single layer.
11. Slide the basket in Air Fryer and select "Air Fry" for 4 minutes.
12. Press "Start/Pause" to begin.
13. Remove from Air Fryer and serve warm.

Nutritional Information per Serving:

- Calories 411
- Total Fat 18.4 g
- Saturated Fat 7.2 g
- Cholesterol 58 mg
- Sodium 912 mg
- Total Carbs 47.3 g
- Fiber 4.9 g
- Sugar 2.4 g
- Protein 15.7 g

Bacon Croquettes

Preparation Time: 15 minutes
Cooking Time: 8 minutes
Servings: 6

Ingredients:

- 1 pound thin bacon slices
- 1 pound sharp cheddar cheese block, cut into 1-inch rectangular pieces
- 1 cup all-purpose flour
- 3 eggs
- 1 cup breadcrumbs
- Salt, as required
- ¼ cup olive oil

Method:

1. Wrap 2 bacon slices around 1 piece of cheddar cheese, covering completely.
2. Repeat with the remaining bacon and cheese pieces.
3. Set the temperature of Ninja Max XL Air Fryer to 390 degrees F and select "Air Fry" to preheat for 5 minutes.
4. Press "Start/Pause" to begin.
5. In a shallow dish, place the flour.
6. In a second shallow dish, beat the eggs.
7. In a third shallow dish, mix together breadcrumbs, salt and oil.
8. Coat the croquettes in flour, then dip into beaten eggs and finally, coat with the breadcrumbs mixture.
9. Arrange the croquettes in the Air Fryer basket in a single layer.
10. Slide the basket in Air Fryer and select "Air Fry" for 8 minutes.
11. Press "Start/Pause" to begin.
12. Remove from Air Fryer and serve warm.

Nutritional Information per Serving:

- Calories 964
- Total Fat 68.4 g
- Saturated Fat 28.5 g
- Cholesterol 244 mg
- Sodium 2000 mg
- Total Carbs 21.1 g
- Fiber 1.4 g
- Sugar 1.7 g
- Protein 45.1 g

Chapter 5: Poultry Recipes

Gingered Drumsticks

Preparation Time: 10 minutes
Cooking Time: 25 minutes
Servings: 3

Ingredients:

- ¼ cup full-fat coconut milk
- 3 teaspoons fresh ginger, minced
- 2 teaspoons ground turmeric
- Salt, as required
- 3 (6-ounce) chicken drumsticks

Method:

1. In a bowl, mix together the coconut milk, ginger and spices.
2. Add the chicken drumsticks and coat with the marinade generously.
3. Refrigerate to marinate for at least 6-8 hours.
4. Set the temperature of Ninja Max XL Air Fryer to 375 degrees F and select "Air Fry" to preheat for 5 minutes.
5. Press "Start/Pause" to begin.
6. Grease the Air Fryer basket.
7. Place chicken drumsticks into the prepared Air Fryer basket in a single layer.
8. Slide the basket in Air Fryer and select "Air Fry" for 25 minutes.
9. Press "Start/Pause" to begin.
10. Remove from Air Fryer and transfer the chicken drumsticks onto a serving platter.
11. Serve hot.

Nutritional Information per Serving:

- Calories 339
- Total Fat 14 g
- Saturated Fat 6.3 g
- Cholesterol 150 mg
- Sodium 193 mg
- Total Carbs 2.9 g
- Fiber 0.5 g
- Sugar 0.4 g
- Protein 47.4 g

Roasted Cornish Game Hen

Preparation Time: 20 minutes
Cooking Time: 16 minutes
Servings: 4

Ingredients:

- ¼ cup olive oil
- 1 teaspoon fresh rosemary, chopped
- 1 teaspoon fresh thyme, chopped
- 1 teaspoon fresh lemon zest, finely grated
- ¼ teaspoon sugar
- ¼ teaspoon red pepper flakes, crushed
- Salt and ground black pepper, as required
- 2 pounds Cornish game hen, backbone removed and halved

Method:

1. In a bowl, mix together oil, herbs, lemon zest, sugar, and spices.
2. Add the hen portions and coat with the marinade generously.
3. Cover and refrigerate for about 24 hours.
4. In a strainer, place the hen portions and set aside to drain any liquid.
5. Set the temperature of Ninja Max XL Air Fryer to 390 degrees F and select "Air Fry" to preheat for 5 minutes.
6. Press "Start/Pause" to begin.
7. Grease the Air Fryer basket.
8. Place hen portions into the prepared Air Fryer basket.
9. Slide the basket in Air Fryer and select "Air Fry" for 16 minutes.
10. Press "Start/Pause" to begin.
11. Remove from the Air Fryer and transfer the hen portions onto a platter.
12. Cut each portion in half and serve.

Nutritional Information per Serving:

- Calories 557
- Total Fat 45.1 g
- Saturated Fat 1.8 g
- Cholesterol 233 mg
- Sodium 181 mg
- Total Carbs 0.8 g
- Fiber 0.37 g
- Sugar 0.3 g
- Protein 38.5 g

Crispy Chicken Legs

Preparation Time: 15 minutes
Cooking Time: 20 minutes
Servings: 3

Ingredients:

- 3 (8-ounce) chicken legs
- 1 cup buttermilk
- 2 cups white flour
- 1 teaspoon garlic powder
- 1 teaspoon onion powder
- 1 teaspoon ground cumin
- 1 teaspoon paprika
- Salt and ground black pepper, as required
- 1 tablespoon olive oil

Method:

1. In a bowl, place the chicken legs and buttermilk and refrigerate for about 2 hours.
2. In a shallow dish, mix together the flour and spices.
3. Remove the chicken from buttermilk.
4. Coat the chicken legs with flour mixture, then dip into buttermilk and finally, coat with the flour mixture again.
5. Set the temperature of Ninja Max XL Air Fryer to 360 degrees F and select "Air Fry" to preheat for 5 minutes.
6. Press "Start/Pause" to begin.
7. Grease the Air Fryer basket.
8. Arrange chicken legs into the prepared Air Fryer basket and drizzle with the oil.
9. Slide the basket in Air Fryer and select "Air Fry" for 20 minutes.
10. Press "Start/Pause" to begin.
11. Remove from Air Fryer and transfer the chicken legs onto serving plates.
12. Serve hot.

Nutritional Information per Serving:

- Calories 817
- Total Fat 23.3 g
- Saturated Fat 5.9 g
- Cholesterol 205 mg
- Sodium 335 mg
- Total Carbs 69.5 g
- Fiber 2.7 g
- Sugar 4.7 g
- Protein 77.4 g

Sweet & Spicy Chicken Drumsticks

Preparation Time: 15 minutes
Cooking Time: 20 minutes
Servings: 4

Ingredients:

- 1 garlic clove, crushed
- 1 tablespoon mustard
- 2 teaspoons brown sugar
- 1 teaspoon cayenne pepper
- 1 teaspoon red chili powder
- Salt and ground black pepper, as required
- 1 tablespoon vegetable oil
- 4 (6-ounce) chicken drumsticks

Method:

1. In a bowl, mix together garlic, mustard, brown sugar, oil, and spices
2. Rub the chicken drumsticks with marinade and refrigerate to marinate for about 20-30 minutes.
3. Set the temperature of Ninja Max XL Air Fryer to 390 degrees F and select "Air Fry" to preheat for 5 minutes.
4. Press "Start/Pause" to begin.
5. Grease the Air Fryer basket.
6. Arrange drumsticks into the prepared Air Fryer basket in a single layer.
7. Slide the basket in Air Fryer and select "Air Fry" for 10 minutes.
8. Press "Start/Pause" to begin.
9. After 10 minutes of cooking, set the temperature of Air Fryer to 300 degrees F for 10 minutes.
10. Remove from Air Fryer and transfer the chicken drumsticks onto a serving platter.
11. Serve hot.

Nutritional Information per Serving:

- Calories 341
- Total Fat 14.1 g
- Saturated Fat 3.3 g
- Cholesterol 150 mg
- Sodium 182 mg
- Total Carbs 3.3 g
- Fiber 0.1.8 0 g
- Protein 47.7 g

Spicy Chicken Legs

Preparation Time: 15 minutes
Cooking Time: 20 minutes
Servings: 4

Ingredients:

- 4 chicken legs
- 3 tablespoons fresh lemon juice
- 3 teaspoons ginger paste
- 3 teaspoons garlic paste
- Salt, as required
- 4 tablespoons plain Yogurt
- 2 teaspoons red chili powder
- 1 teaspoon ground cumin
- 1 teaspoon ground coriander
- 1 teaspoon ground turmeric
- Ground black pepper, as required

Method:

1. In a bowl, mix together the chicken legs, lemon juice, ginger, garlic and salt. Set aside for about 15 minutes.
2. Meanwhile, in another bowl, mix together the yogurt and spices.
3. Add the chicken legs and coat with the spice mixture generously.
4. Cover the bowl and refrigerate for at least 10-12 hours.
5. Set the temperature of Ninja Max XL Air Fryer to 445 degrees F and select "Air Fry" to preheat for 5 minutes.
6. Press "Start/Pause" to begin.
7. Line the Air Fryer basket with a piece of foil.
8. Arrange chicken legs into the prepared Air Fryer basket.
9. Slide the basket in Air Fryer and select "Air Fry" for 18-20 minutes.
10. Press "Start/Pause" to begin.
11. Remove from Air Fryer and transfer the chicken legs onto serving plates.
12. Serve hot.

Nutritional Information per Serving:

- Calories 461
- Total Fat 17.6 g
- Saturated Fat 5 g
- Cholesterol 203 mg
- Sodium 262 mg
- Total Carbs 4.3 g
- Fiber 0.9 g
- Sugar 1.5 g
- Protein 67.1 g

Marinated Chicken Thighs

Preparation Time: 10 minutes
Cooking Time: 30 minutes
Servings: 4

Ingredients:

- 4 (6-ounce) bone-in, skin-on chicken thighs
- Salt and ground black pepper, as required
- ½ cup Italian salad dressing
- 1 teaspoon onion powder
- 1 teaspoon garlic powder

Method:

1. Season the chicken thighs with salt and black pepper evenly.
2. In a large bowl, add the chicken thighs and dressing and mix well.
3. Cover the bowl and refrigerate to marinate overnight.
4. Remove the chicken breast from the bowl and place onto a plate.
5. Sprinkle the chicken thighs with onion powder and garlic powder.
6. Set the temperature of Ninja Max XL Air Fryer to 360 degrees F and select "Air Fry" to preheat for 5 minutes.
7. Press "Start/Pause" to begin.
8. Grease the Air Fryer basket.
9. Arrange the chicken thighs into the prepared Air Fryer basket.
10. Slide the basket in Air Fryer and select "Air Fry" for 30 minutes.
11. Press "Start/Pause" to begin.
12. After 15 minutes of cooking, flip the chicken thighs once.
13. Remove from Air Fryer and transfer the chicken thighs onto serving plates.
14. Serve hot.

Nutritional Information per Serving:

- Calories 413
- Total Fat 21 g
- Saturated Fat 4.8 g
- Cholesterol 171 mg
- Sodium 194 mg
- Total Carbs 4.1 g
- Fiber 0.1 g
- Sugar 2.8 g
- Protein 49.5 g

Stuffed Chicken Breasts

Preparation Time: 15 minutes
Cooking Time: 30 minutes
Servings: 2

Ingredients:

- 1 tablespoon olive oil
- 1¾ ounces fresh spinach
- ¼ cup ricotta cheese, shredded
- 2 (4-ounce) skinless, boneless chicken breasts
- Salt and ground black pepper, as required
- 2 tablespoons Parmesan cheese, grated
- ¼ teaspoon paprika

Method:

1. In a medium skillet, heat the oil over medium heat and cook the spinach for about 3-4 minutes.
2. Stir in the ricotta and cook for about 40-60 seconds.
3. Remove the skillet from heat and set aside to cool.
4. Cut slits into the chicken breasts about ¼-inch apart but not all the way through.
5. Stuff each chicken breast with the spinach mixture.
6. Season each chicken breast with salt and black pepper and then sprinkle the top with Parmesan cheese and paprika.
7. Set the temperature of Ninja Max XL Air Fryer to 390 degrees F and select "Air Fry" to preheat for 5 minutes.
8. Press "Start/Pause" to begin.
9. Grease the Air Fryer basket.
10. Arrange the chicken breasts into the prepared basket in a single layer.
11. Slide the basket in Air Fryer and select "Air Fry" for 25 minutes.
12. Press "Start/Pause" to begin.
13. Remove from Air Fryer and transfer the chicken breasts onto a serving platter.
14. Serve hot.

Nutritional Information per Serving:

- Calories 269
- Total Fat 14.8 g
- Saturated Fat 4.7 g
- Cholesterol 79 mg
- Sodium 219 mg
- Total Carbs 2.6 g
- Fiber 0.7 g
- Sugar 0.2 g
- Protein 31.6 g

Glazed Turkey Breast

Preparation Time: 15 minutes
Cooking Time: 55 minutes
Servings: 10

Ingredients:

- 1 teaspoon dried thyme, crushed
- ½ teaspoon dried sage, crushed
- ½ teaspoon smoked paprika
- Salt and ground black pepper, as required
- 1 (5-pound) boneless turkey breast
- 2 teaspoons olive oil
- ¼ cup maple syrup
- 2 tablespoons Dijon mustard
- 1 tablespoon butter, softened

Method:

1. In a bowl, mix together the herbs, paprika, salt, and black pepper.
2. Coat the turkey breast with oil evenly.
3. Now, coat the outer side of turkey breast with herb mixture.
4. Set the temperature of Ninja Max XL Air Fryer to 350 degrees F and select "Air Fry" to preheat for 5 minutes.
5. Press "Start/Pause" to begin.
6. Grease the Air Fryer basket.
7. Place turkey breast into the prepared Air Fryer basket.
8. Slide the basket in Air Fryer and select "Air Fry" for 55 minutes.
9. While cooking, flip the turkey breast once after 25 minutes and then after 37 minutes.
10. Meanwhile, in a bowl, mix together the maple syrup, mustard, and butter.
11. After 50 minutes of cooking, press "Start/Pause" to pause cooking.
12. Remove the basket from Air Fryer and coat the turkey breast with glaze evenly.
13. Again, slide the basket in Air Fryer and press "Start/Pause" to resume cooking.
14. Remove from Air Fryer and place the turkey breast onto a cutting board for about 10 minutes before slicing.
15. With a sharp knife, cut the turkey breast into desired sized slices and serve.

Nutritional Information per Serving:

- Calories 302
- Total Fat 3.3 g
- Saturated Fat 0.9 g
- Cholesterol 143 mg
- Sodium 170 mg
- Total Carbs 5.6 g
- Fiber 0.2 g
- Sugar 4.7 g
- Protein 56.2 g

Lemony Chicken Thighs

Preparation Time: 15 minutes
Cooking Time: 20 minutes
Servings: 6

Ingredients:

- 6 (6-ounce) chicken thighs
- 2 tablespoons olive oil
- 2 tablespoons fresh lemon juice
- 1 tablespoon Italian seasoning
- Salt and ground black pepper, as required
- 1 lemon, sliced thinly

Method:

1. In a large bowl, add all the ingredients except for lemon slices and toss to coat well.
2. Refrigerate to marinate for 30 minutes to overnight.
3. Remove the chicken thighs and let any excess marinade drip off.
4. Set the temperature of Ninja Max XL Air Fryer to 350 degrees F and select "Air Fry" to preheat for 5 minutes.
5. Press "Start/Pause" to begin.
6. Grease the Air Fryer basket.
7. Arrange the chicken thighs in the prepared Air Fryer basket.
8. Slide the basket in Air Fryer and select "Air Fry" for 20 minutes.
9. Press "Start/Pause" to begin.
10. After 10 minutes of cooking, flip the chicken thighs.
11. Remove from Air Fryer and transfer the chicken thighs onto serving plates.
12. Serve hot alongside the lemon slices.

Nutritional Information per Serving:

- Calories 372
- Total Fat 18 g
- Saturated Fat 4.3 g
- Cholesterol 153 mg
- Sodium 175 mg
- Total Carbs 0.6 g
- Fiber 0.1 g
- Sugar 0.4 g
- Protein 49.3 g

Glazed Chicken Drumsticks

Preparation Time: 15 minutes
Cooking Time: 22 minutes
Servings: 4

Ingredients:

- ¼ cup Dijon mustard
- 1 tablespoon honey
- 2 tablespoons olive oil
- ½ tablespoon fresh rosemary, minced
- 1 tablespoon fresh thyme, minced
- Salt and ground black pepper, as required
- 4 (6-ounce) chicken drumsticks

Method:

1. In a bowl, mix together the mustard, honey, oil, herbs, salt, and black pepper.
2. Add the drumsticks and coat with the mixture generously.
3. Cover and refrigerate to marinate overnight.
4. Set the temperature of Ninja Max XL Air Fryer to 320 degrees F and select "Air Fry" to preheat for 5 minutes.
5. Press "Start/Pause" to begin.
6. Grease the Air Fryer basket.
7. Arrange the chicken drumsticks into the prepared Air Fryer basket in a single layer.
8. Slide the basket in Air Fryer and select "Air Fry" for 12 minutes.
9. Press "Start/Pause" to begin.
10. After 10 minutes of cooking, set the temperature of Air Fryer to 355 degrees F for 10 minutes.
11. Remove from Air Fryer and transfer the chicken drumsticks onto a serving platter.
12. Serve hot.

Nutritional Information per Serving:

- Calories 377
- Total Fat 17.5 g
- Saturated Fat 3.7 g
- Cholesterol 150 mg
- Sodium 353 mg
- Total Carbs 5.9 g
- Fiber 1 g
- Sugar 4.5 g
- Protein 47.6 g

Roasted Chicken

Preparation Time: 15 minutes
Cooking Time: 1 hour
Servings: 2

Ingredients:

- 1 (1½-pound) whole chicken
- Salt and ground black pepper, as required
- 1 tablespoon olive oil
- ½ pound small potatoes

Method:

1. Set the temperature of Ninja Max XL Air Fryer to 390 degrees F and select "Air Fry" to preheat for 5 minutes.
2. Press "Start/Pause" to begin. Grease the Air Fryer basket.
3. Season the chicken with salt and black pepper.
4. Place chicken into the prepared Air Fryer basket.
5. Slide the basket in Air Fryer and select "Air Fry" for 60 minutes.
6. Press "Start/Pause" to begin.
7. Meanwhile, in a bowl, add the potatoes, oil, salt, and black pepper and toss to coat well.
8. After 40 minutes of cooking, press "Start/Pause" to pause cooking.
9. Place the potatoes into the prepared Air Fryer basket alongside the chicken.
10. Again, slide the basket in Air Fryer and Press "Start/Pause" to resume cooking.
11. Remove from the Air Fryer and transfer potatoes into a bowl.
12. Place the chicken onto a cutting board for about 10 minutes.
13. Cut the chicken into desired size pieces and serve alongside the potatoes.

Nutritional Information per Serving:

- Calories 776
- Total Fat 49.6 g
- Saturated Fat 13.2 g
- Cholesterol 289 mg
- Sodium 358 mg
- Total Carbs 17.8 g
- Fiber 2.7 g
- Sugar 1.3 g
- Protein 62.7 g

Chicken Kabobs

Preparation Time: 15 minutes
Cooking Time: 9 minutes
Servings: 2

Ingredients:

- 1 (8-ounce) chicken breast, cut into medium-sized pieces
- 1 tablespoon fresh lemon juice
- 3 garlic cloves, grated
- 1 tablespoon fresh oregano, minced
- ½ teaspoon lemon zest, grated
- Salt and ground black pepper, as required
- 1 teaspoon plain Greek yogurt
- 1 teaspoon olive oil

Method:

1. In a large bowl, add the chicken, lemon juice, garlic, oregano, lemon zest, salt and black pepper and toss to coat well.
2. Cover the bowl and refrigerate overnight.
3. Remove the bowl from refrigerator and stir in the yogurt and oil.
4. Thread the chicken pieces onto the metal skewers.
5. Set the temperature of Ninja Max XL Air Fryer to 350 degrees F and select "Air Fry" to preheat for 5 minutes.
6. Press "Start/Pause" to begin.
7. Grease the Air Fryer basket.
8. Arrange the skewers into the prepared basket in a single layer.
9. Slide the basket in Air Fryer and select "Air Fry" for 9 minutes.
10. Press "Start/Pause" to begin.
11. While cooking flip the skewers once halfway through.
12. Remove from Air Fryer and transfer the kabobs onto a serving platter.
13. Serve hot.

Nutritional Information per Serving:

- Calories 167
- Total Fat 5.5 g
- Saturated Fat 0.5 g
- Cholesterol 73 mg
- Sodium 140 mg
- Total Carbs 3.4 g
- Fiber 1.1 g
- Sugar 0.5 g
- Protein 24.8 g

Turkey Burgers

Preparation Time: 15 minutes
Cooking Time: 15 minutes
Servings: 2

Ingredients:

- 8 ounces ground turkey breast
- 1½ tablespoons extra-virgin olive oil
- 2 garlic cloves, grated
- 2 teaspoons fresh oregano, chopped
- ½ teaspoon red pepper flakes, crushed
- Salt, as required
- ¼ cup feta cheese, crumbled

Method:

1. In a large bowl, add all the ingredients except for cheese and mix until well combined.
2. Make 2 (½-inch-thick) patties from the mixture.
3. Set the temperature of Ninja Max XL Air Fryer to 360 degrees F and select "Air Fry" to preheat for 5 minutes.
4. Press "Start/Pause" to begin.
5. Grease the Air Fryer basket.
6. Arrange the patties into the prepared Air Fryer basket.
7. Slide the basket in Air Fryer and select "Air Fry" for 15 minutes.
8. Press "Start/Pause" to begin.
9. While cooking, flip the patties once halfway through.
10. Remove from Air Fryer and transfer the patties onto serving plates.
11. Serve hot with the topping of feta.

Nutritional Information per Serving:

- Calories 364
- Total Fat 23.133 g
- Saturated Fat 6.7 g
- Cholesterol 101 mg
- Sodium 359 mg
- Total Carbs 3 g
- Fiber 0.8 g
- Sugar 0.9 g
- Protein 35.6 g

Oat Crusted Chicken Breasts

Preparation Time: 15 minutes
Cooking Time: 12 minutes
Servings: 2

Ingredients:

- 2 (6-ounce) chicken breasts
- Salt and ground black pepper, as required
- ¾ cup oats
- 2 tablespoons mustard powder
- 1 tablespoon fresh parsley
- 2 medium eggs

Method:

1. Place the chicken breasts onto a cutting board and with a meat mallet, flatten each into even thickness.
2. Then, cut each breast in half.
3. Sprinkle the chicken pieces with salt and black pepper and set aside.
4. In a blender, add the oats, mustard powder, parsley, salt and black pepper and pulse until a coarse breadcrumb-like mixture is formed.
5. Transfer the oat mixture into a shallow bowl.
6. In another bowl, crack the eggs and beat well.
7. Coat the chicken with oats mixture and then, dip into beaten eggs and again, coat with the oats mixture.
8. Set the temperature of Ninja Max XL Air Fryer to 350 degrees F and select "Air Fry" to preheat for 5 minutes.
9. Press "Start/Pause" to begin.
10. Grease the Air Fryer pan.
11. Arrange chicken breasts into the prepared pan in a single layer.
12. Slide the pan in Air Fryer and select "Air Fry" for 12 minutes.
13. Press "Start/Pause" to begin.
14. While cooking, flip the chicken breasts once halfway through.
15. Remove from Air Fryer and transfer the chicken breasts onto a serving platter.
16. Serve hot.

Nutritional Information per Serving:

- Calories 556
- Total Fat 22.2 g
- Saturated Fat 5.3 g
- Cholesterol 315 mg
- Sodium 289 mg
- Total Carbs 25.1 g
- Fiber 4.8 g
- Sugar 1.40 g
- Protein 61.6 g

Parmesan Chicken Breasts

Preparation Time: 15 minutes
Cooking Time: 22 minutes
Servings: 2

Ingredients:

- 2 (6-ounce) chicken breasts
- 1 egg, beaten
- 4 ounces breadcrumbs
- 1 tablespoon fresh basil
- 2 tablespoons olive oil
- ¼ cup pasta sauce
- ¼ cup Parmesan cheese, grated

Method:

1. In a shallow bowl, beat the egg.
2. In another bowl, add the oil, breadcrumbs, and basil and mix until a crumbly mixture forms.
3. Now, dip each chicken breast into the beaten egg and then, coat with the breadcrumb mixture.
4. Set the temperature of Ninja Max XL Air Fryer to 350 degrees F and select "Air Fry" to preheat for 5 minutes.
5. Press "Start/Pause" to begin.
6. Grease the Air Fryer basket.
7. Arrange chicken breasts into the prepared basket
8. Slide the basket in Air Fryer and select "Air Fry" for 22 minutes.
9. Press "Start/Pause" to begin.
10. After 15 minutes of cooking, press "Start/Pause" to pause cooking.
11. Remove the basket from Air Fryer and spoon the pasta sauce over chicken breasts, followed by the cheese.
12. Again, slide the basket in Air Fryer and press "Start/Pause" to resume cooking.
13. Remove from Air Fryer and transfer the chicken breasts onto a serving platter.
14. Serve hot.

Nutritional Information per Serving:

- Calories 768
- Total Fat 35.4 g
- Saturated Fat 8.8 g
- Cholesterol 241 mg
- Sodium 890 mg
- Total Carbs 45.7 g
- Fiber 3.4 g
- Sugar 6.5 g
- Protein 63.9 g

Chapter 6: Seafood Recipes

Simple Salmon

Preparation Time: 10 minutes
Cooking Time: 10 minutes
Servings: 2

Ingredients:

- 2 (6-ounce) salmon fillets
- Salt and ground black pepper, as required
- 1 tablespoon olive oil

Method:

1. Set the temperature of Ninja Max XL Air Fryer to 360 degrees F and select "Air Fry" to preheat for 5 minutes.
2. "Start/Pause" to begin.
3. Grease the Air Fryer basket.
4. Season each salmon fillet with salt and black pepper and then, coat with the oil.
5. Arrange salmon fillets into the prepared Air Fryer basket in a single layer.
6. Slide the basket in Air Fryer and select "Air Fry" for 10 minutes.
7. Press "Start/Pause" to begin.
8. Remove from Air Fryer and place the salmon fillets onto the serving plates.
9. Serve hot.

Nutritional Information per Serving:

- Calories 285
- Total Fat 17.5 g
- Saturated Fat 2.5 g
- Cholesterol 75 mg
- Sodium 153 mg
- Total Carbs 0 g
- Fiber 0 g
- Sugar 0 g
- Protein 33 g

Crispy Cod

Preparation Time: 15 minutes
Cooking Time: 15 minutes
Servings: 4

Ingredients:

- 4 (4-ounce) (¾-inch thick) cod fillets
- Salt, as required
- 2 tablespoons all-purpose flour
- 2 eggs
- ½ cup panko breadcrumbs
- 1 teaspoon fresh dill, minced
- ½ teaspoon dry mustard
- ½ teaspoon lemon zest, grated
- ½ teaspoon onion powder
- ½ teaspoon paprika
- Olive oil cooking spray

Method:

1. Season the cod fillets with salt generously.
2. In a shallow bowl, place the flour.
3. Crack the eggs in a second bowl and beat well.
4. In a third bowl, mix together the panko, dill, lemon zest, mustard and spices.
5. Coat each cod fillet with the flour, then dip into beaten eggs and finally, coat with panko mixture.
6. Set the temperature of Ninja Max XL Air Fryer to 400 degrees F and select "Air Fry" to preheat for 5 minutes.
7. Press "Start/Pause" to begin.
8. Grease the Air Fryer basket.
9. Arrange the cod fillets into the Air Fryer basket and spray the tops with cooking spray.
10. Slide the basket in Air Fryer and select "Air Fry" for 15 minutes.
11. While cooking, flip the cod fillets once hallway through.
12. Remove from Air Fryer and transfer the cod fillets onto serving plates.
13. Serve hot.

Nutritional Information per Serving:

- Calories 190
- Total Fat 4.3 g
- Saturated Fat 1.1 g
- Cholesterol 138 mg
- Sodium 141 mg
- Total Carbs 5.9 g
- Fiber 0.4 g
- Sugar 0.4 g
- Protein 24 g

Cod Parcel

Preparation Time: 15 minutes
Cooking Time: 15 minutes
Servings: 4

Ingredients:

- 2 tablespoons butter, melted
- 1 tablespoon fresh lemon juice
- ½ teaspoon dried tarragon
- Salt and ground black pepper, as required
- ½ cup red bell peppers, seeded and thinly sliced
- ½ cup carrots, peeled and julienned
- ½ cup fennel bulbs, julienned
- 2 (5-ounce) frozen cod fillets, thawed
- 1 tablespoon olive oil

Method:

1. In a large bowl, mix well butter, lemon juice, tarragon, salt, and black pepper.
2. Add the bell pepper, carrot, and fennel bulb and generously coat with the mixture.
3. Arrange 2 large parchment squares onto a smooth surface.
4. Coat the cod fillets with oil and then, sprinkle with salt and black pepper.
5. Arrange 1 cod fillet onto each parchment square and top each evenly with the vegetables.
6. Top with any remaining sauce from the bowl.
7. Fold the parchment paper and crimp the sides to secure fish and vegetables.
8. Set the temperature of Ninja Max XL Air Fryer to 350 degrees F and select "Air Fry" to preheat for 5 minutes.
9. Press "Start/Pause" to begin.
10. Arrange fish parcels into the Air Fryer basket.
11. Slide the basket in Air Fryer and select "Air Fry" for 15 minutes.
12. Press "Start/Pause" to begin.
13. Remove from Air Fryer and place the parcels onto serving plates.
14. Carefully, open each parcel and serve warm.

Nutritional Information per Serving:

- Calories 306
- Total Fat 20 g
- Saturated Fat 8.4 g
- Cholesterol 100 mg
- Sodium 281 mg
- Total Carbs 6.8 g
- Fiber 1.8 g
- Sugar 3 g
- Protein 26.3 g

Salmon with Asparagus

Preparation Time: 15 minutes
Cooking Time: 11 minutes
Servings: 2

Ingredients:

- 2 (6-ounce) boneless salmon fillets
- 1½ tablespoons fresh lemon juice
- 1 tablespoon olive oil
- 2 tablespoons fresh parsley, roughly chopped
- 2 tablespoons fresh dill, roughly chopped
- 8 ounces asparagus
- Salt and ground black pepper, as required

Method:

1. In a small bowl, mix together the lemon juice, oil, herbs, salt, and black pepper.
2. In a large bowl, mix together the salmon and ¾ of oil mixture.
3. In a second large bowl, add the asparagus and remaining oil mixture and mix well.
4. Set the temperature of Ninja Max XL Air Fryer to 400 degrees F and select "Air Fry" to preheat for 5 minutes.
5. Press "Start/Pause" to begin.
6. Grease the Air Fryer basket.
7. Arrange asparagus into the prepared Air Fryer basket.
8. Slide the basket in Air Fryer and select "Air Fry" for 11 minutes.
9. Press "Start/Pause" to begin.
10. After 3 minutes of cooking, press "Start/Pause" to pause cooking.
11. Remove the basket from Air Fryer and arrange the salmon fillets on top of asparagus.
12. Again, slide the basket in Air Fryer and press "Start/Pause" to resume cooking.
13. Remove from Air Fryer and place the salmon fillets onto serving plates.
14. Serve hot alongside the asparagus.

Nutritional Information per Serving:

- Calories 320
- Total Fat 17.9 g
- Saturated Fat 2.7 g
- Cholesterol 75183 mg
- Sodium 166 mg
- Total Carbs 6.6 g
- Fiber 3 g
- Sugar 2.4 g
- Protein 36.3 g

Salmon with Green Beans

Preparation Time: 15 minutes
Cooking Time: 12 minutes
Servings: 4

Ingredients:

For Green Beans:

- 5 cups frozen green beans
- 1 tablespoon olive oil
- Salt, as required

For Salmon:

- 2 garlic cloves, minced
- 2 tablespoons fresh dill, chopped
- 2 tablespoons fresh lemon juice
- 1 tablespoon olive oil
- Salt, as required
- 4 (6-ounce) salmon fillets

Method:

1. Set the temperature of Ninja Max XL Air Fryer to 375 degrees F and select "Air Fry" to preheat for 5 minutes.
2. Press "Start/Pause" to begin.
3. Grease the Air Fryer basket.
4. In a large bowl, mix together the green beans, oil, and salt.
5. Arrange the green beans into the prepared Air Fryer basket.
6. Slide the basket in Air Fryer and select "Air Fry" for 12 minutes.
7. Meanwhile, for salmon: in a bowl, mix together the garlic, dill, lemon juice, olive oil and salt.
8. After 6 minutes of cooking, press "Start/Pause" to pause cooking.
9. Remove the basket from Air Fryer and flip the green beans.
10. Arrange the salmon fillets on top of asparagus.
11. Place the garlic mixture on top of each salmon fillet evenly.
12. Again, slide the basket in Air Fryer and press "Start/Pause" to resume cooking.
13. Remove from Air Fryer and place the salmon fillets onto serving plates.
14. Serve hot alongside the green beans.

Nutritional Information per Serving:

- Calories 336
- Total Fat 17.8 g
- Saturated Fat 2.6 g
- Cholesterol 75 mg
- Sodium 127 mg
- Total Carbs 11.3 g
- Fiber 5 g
- Sugar 2.1 g
- Protein 36 g

Haddock with Pesto

Preparation Time: 15 minutes
Cooking Time: 8 minutes
Servings: 2

Ingredients:

- 2 (6-ounce) haddock fillets
- 1/3 cup plus 1 tablespoon olive oil, divided
- Salt and ground black pepper, as required
- 2 tablespoons pine nuts
- 3 tablespoons fresh basil, chopped
- 1 tablespoon Parmesan cheese, grated

Method:

1. Set the temperature of Ninja Max XL Air Fryer to 355 degrees F and select "Air Fry" to preheat for 5 minutes.
2. Press "Start/Pause" to begin.
3. Grease the Air Fryer basket.
4. Coat the fish fillets with 1 tablespoon of oil and then sprinkle with salt and black pepper.
5. Arrange fish fillets into the prepared Air Fryer basket in a single layer.
6. Slide the basket in Air Fryer and select "Air Fry" for 8 minutes.
7. Press "Start/Pause" to begin.
8. Meanwhile, for the pesto: add the remaining ingredients in a food processor and pulse until smooth.
9. Remove from Air Fryer and transfer the flounder fillets onto serving plates.
10. Top with the pesto and serve.

Nutritional Information per Serving:

- Calories 699
- Total Fat 58.5 g
- Saturated Fat 9 g
- Cholesterol 133 mg
- Sodium 416 mg
- Total Carbs 1.7 g
- Fiber 0.4 g
- Sugar 0.3 g
- Protein 45.5 g

Scallops in Butter Sauce

Preparation Time: 15 minutes
Cooking Time: 6 minutes
Servings: 2

Ingredients:

- 10 (1-ounce) sea scallops, cleaned and patted very dry
- Salt and ground black pepper, as required
- 3 tablespoons butter, melted
- 2 tablespoons fresh parsley, chopped finely
- 2 teaspoons capers, chopped finely
- 1 teaspoon fresh lemon zest, grated finely
- ½ teaspoon garlic, chopped finely

Method:

1. Season each scallop with salt and black pepper evenly.
2. Set the temperature of Ninja Max XL Air Fryer to 400 degrees F and select "Air Fry" to preheat for 5 minutes.
3. Press "Start/Pause" to begin.
4. Grease the Air Fryer basket.
5. Arrange the scallops into the prepared Air Fryer basket in a single layer.
6. Slide the basket in Air Fryer and select "Air Fry" for 6 minutes.
7. Press "Start/Pause" to begin.
8. Meanwhile, for the sauce: in a bowl, mix the remaining ingredients.
9. Remove from Air Fryer and transfer the scallops onto serving plates.
10. Top with the sauce and serve immediately.

Nutritional Information per Serving:

- Calories 281
- Total Fat 18.4 g
- Saturated Fat 11.1 g
- Cholesterol 93 mg
- Sodium 516 mg
- Total Carbs 4.2 g
- Fiber 0.3 g
- Sugar 0.1 g
- Protein 24.2 g

Salmon Cakes

Preparation Time: 2 minutes
Cooking Time: 27 minutes
Servings: 6

Ingredients:

- 3 large russet potatoes, peeled and cubed
- 1 (6-ounce) salmon fillet
- 1 egg
- ¾ cup frozen vegetables (of your choice), parboiled and drained
- 2 tablespoons fresh parsley, chopped
- 1 teaspoon fresh dill, chopped
- Salt and ground black pepper, as required
- 1 cup breadcrumbs
- ¼ cup olive oil

Method:

1. In a pan of boiling water, cook the potatoes for about 10 minutes.
2. Drain the potatoes well.
3. Transfer the potatoes into a bowl and with a potato masher, mash them. Set aside to cool completely.
4. Set the temperature of Ninja Max XL Air Fryer to 355 degrees F and select "Air Fry" to preheat for 5 minutes.
5. Press "Start/Pause" to begin.
6. Grease the Air Fryer basket.
7. Arrange the salmon fillet into the prepared Air Fryer basket.
8. Slide the basket in Air Fryer and select "Air Fry" for 5 minutes.
9. Remove from Air Fryer and transfer the salmon fillet into a large bowl.
10. With a fork, flake the salmon.
11. Add the mashed potatoes, egg, vegetables, herbs, salt, and black pepper into the bowl of salmon and mix until well combined.
12. Make 6 equal-sized patties from the mixture.
13. Coat the patties with breadcrumbs and then, drizzle with the oil.
14. Again, set the temperature of Ninja Max XL Air Fryer to 355 degrees F and select "Air Fry" to preheat for 5 minutes.
15. Press "Start/Pause" to begin.
16. Line the Air Fryer basket with a lightly greased piece of foil.
17. Arrange the patties into the prepared Air Fryer basket in a single layer.
18. Slide the basket in Air Fryer and select "Air Fry" for 10-12 minutes.
19. Press "Start/Pause" to begin.
20. While cooking, flip the patties once halfway through.
21. Remove from Air Fryer and place the patties onto serving plates.

22. Serve warm.

Nutritional Information per Serving:

- Calories 330
- Total Fat 12.1 g
- Saturated Fat 2 g
- Cholesterol 40 mg
- Sodium 262 mg

- Total Carbs 44.4 g
- Fiber 6.5 g
- Sugar 3.3 g
- Protein 12.4 g

Spiced Salmon

Preparation Time: 10 minutes
Cooking Time: 11 minutes
Servings: 2

Ingredients:

- 1 teaspoon smoked paprika
- 1 teaspoon cayenne pepper
- 1 teaspoon onion powder
- 1 teaspoon garlic powder
- Salt and ground black pepper, as required
- 2 (6-ounce) (1½-inch thick) salmon fillets
- 2 teaspoons olive oil

Method:

1. In a bowl, add the spices and mix well.
2. Drizzle the salmon fillets with oil and then rub with the spice mixture.
3. Set the temperature of Ninja Max XL Air Fryer to 390 degrees F and select "Air Fry" to preheat for 5 minutes.
4. Press "Start/Pause" to begin.
5. Grease the Air Fryer basket.
6. Arrange salmon fillets into the prepared Air Fryer basket in a single layer.
7. Slide the basket in Air Fryer and select "Air Fry" for 11 minutes.
8. Press "Start/Pause" to begin.
9. Remove from Air Fryer and place the salmon fillets onto the serving plates.
10. Serve hot.

Nutritional Information per Serving:

- Calories 280
- Total Fat 15.5 g
- Saturated Fat 2.2 g
- Cholesterol 75 mg
- Sodium 154 mg
- Total Carbs 32.1 g
- Fiber 0.8 g
- Sugar 1 g
- Protein 33.6 g

Cheesy Shrimp

Preparation Time: 20 minutes
Cooking Time: 20 minutes
Servings: 6

Ingredients:

- 2/3 cup Parmesan cheese, grated
- 4 garlic cloves, minced
- 2 tablespoons olive oil
- 1 teaspoon dried basil
- ½ teaspoon dried oregano
- 1 teaspoon onion powder
- ½ teaspoon red pepper flakes, crushed
- Ground black pepper, as required
- 2 pounds shrimp, peeled and deveined
- 1-2 tablespoons fresh lemon juice

Method:

1. In a large bowl, mix together the Parmesan cheese, garlic, oil, herbs, and spices.
2. Add the shrimp and toss to coat.
3. Set the temperature of Ninja Max XL Air Fryer to 350 degrees F and select "Air Fry" to preheat for 5 minutes.
4. "Start/Pause" to begin.
5. Grease the Air Fryer basket.
6. Arrange shrimp into the prepared Air Fryer basket in a single layer in 2 batches.
7. Slide the basket in Air Fryer and select "Air Fry" for 10 minutes.
8. Press "Start/Pause" to begin.
9. Remove from Air Fryer and transfer the shrimp onto serving plates.
10. Drizzle with lemon juice and serve immediately.

Nutritional Information per Serving:

- Calories 258
- Total Fat 9.4 g
- Saturated Fat 2.5 g
- Cholesterol 326 mg
- Sodium 447 mg
- Total Carbs 3.5 g
- Fiber 0.2 g
- Sugar 0.2 g
- Protein 38.2 g

Seafood with Pasta

Preparation Time: 2 minutes
Cooking Time: 18 minutes
Servings: 4

Ingredients:

- 14 ounces pasta (of your choice)
- 4 tablespoons pesto, divided
- 4 (4-ounce) salmon steaks
- 2 tablespoons olive oil
- ½ pound cherry tomatoes, chopped
- 8 large prawns, peeled and deveined
- 2 tablespoons fresh lemon juice
- 2 tablespoons fresh thyme, chopped

Method:

1. In a large pan of the salted boiling water, add the pasta and cook for about 8-10 minutes or until desired doneness.
2. Drain the pasta and transfer into a large bowl. Set aside.
3. Set the temperature of Ninja Max XL Air Fryer to 390 degrees F and select "Air Fry" to preheat for 5 minutes.
4. Press "Start/Pause" to begin.
5. Meanwhile, in the bottom of a baking dish, spread 1 tablespoon of pesto.
6. Place the salmon steaks and tomatoes over pesto in a single layer and drizzle evenly with the oil.
7. Now, add the prawns on top in a single layer.
8. Drizzle with lemon juice and sprinkle with thyme.
9. Arrange the baking dish in Air Fryer and select "Air Fry" for 8 minutes.
10. Press "Start/Pause" to begin.
11. Remove the salmon mixture from Air Fryer.
12. Add the remaining pesto and toss to coat well.
13. Divide the pasta onto serving plates and top with salmon mixture.
14. Serve immediately.

Nutritional Information per Serving:

- Calories 592
- Total Fat 23.2 g
- Saturated Fat 3.8 g
- Cholesterol 149 mg
- Sodium 203 mg
- Total Carbs 58.7 g
- Fiber 1.5 g
- Sugar 2.7 g
- Protein 37.9 g

Crispy Flounder

Preparation Time: 15 minutes
Cooking Time: 12 minutes
Servings: 3

Ingredients:

- 1 egg
- 1 cup dry Italian breadcrumbs
- ¼ cup olive oil
- 3 (6-ounce) flounder fillets
- 1 lemon, sliced

Method:

1. In a shallow bowl, beat the egg
2. In another bowl, add the breadcrumbs and oil and mix until a crumbly mixture is formed.
3. Dip the flounder fillets into the beaten egg and then, coat with the breadcrumb mixture.
4. Set the temperature of Ninja Max XL Air Fryer to 356 degrees F and select "Air Fry" to preheat for 5 minutes.
5. Press "Start/Pause" to begin.
6. Grease the Air Fryer basket.
7. Arrange flounder fillets into the prepared Air Fryer basket in a single layer.
8. Slide the basket in Air Fryer and select "Air Fry" for 12 minutes.
9. Press "Start/Pause" to begin.
10. Remove from Air Fryer and transfer the flounder fillets onto serving plates.
11. Garnish with the lemon slices and serve hot.

Nutritional Information per Serving:

- Calories 508
- Total Fat 22.8 g
- Saturated Fat 3.9 g
- Cholesterol 170 mg
- Sodium 463 mg
- Total Carbs 26.5 g
- Fiber 1.8 g
- Sugar 2.5 g
- Protein 47.8 g

Seasoned Tilapia

Preparation Time: 10 minutes
Cooking Time: 12 minutes
Servings: 2

Ingredients:

- ½ teaspoon lemon pepper seasoning
- ½ teaspoon garlic powder
- ½ teaspoon onion powder
- Salt and ground black pepper, as required
- 2 (6-ounce) tilapia fillets
- 1 lemon, cut into wedges

Method:

1. In a small bowl, mix together the lemon pepper seasoning, garlic powder, onion powder, salt and black pepper.
2. Rub the fish fillets with seasoning mixture generously.
3. Set the temperature of Ninja Max XL Air Fryer to 360 degrees F and select "Air Fry" to preheat for 5 minutes.
4. Press "Start/Pause" to begin.
5. Line the Air Fryer basket with a greased piece of parchment paper.
6. Arrange the fish fillets into the prepared Air Fryer basket in a single layer.
7. Place the lemon slices over fish fillets.
8. Slide the basket in Air Fryer and select "Air Fry" for 12 minutes.
9. Press "Start/Pause" to begin.
10. Remove from Air Fryer and transfer the fish fillets onto serving plates.
11. Serve hot.

Nutritional Information per Serving:

- Calories 148
- Total Fat 1.6 g
- Saturated Fat 0.7 g
- Cholesterol 83 mg
- Sodium 139 mg
- Total Carbs 2 g
- Fiber 0.5 g
- Sugar 0.6 g
- Protein 32 g

Shrimp Scampi

Preparation Time: 20 minutes
Cooking Time: 7 minutes
Servings: 3

Ingredients:

- 4 tablespoons salted butter
- 1 tablespoon fresh lemon juice
- 1 tablespoon garlic, minced
- 2 teaspoons red pepper flakes, crushed
- 1 pound shrimp, peeled and deveined
- 2 tablespoons fresh basil, chopped
- 1 tablespoon fresh chives, chopped
- 2 tablespoons dry white wine

Method:

1. Arrange a 7-inch round baking pan in the Air Fryer basket.
2. Slide the basket in Air Fryer and set the temperature of Ninja Max XL Air Fryer to 325 degrees F.
3. Select "Air Fry" to preheat for 5 minutes and press "Start/Pause" to begin.
4. Carefully remove the hot pan from Air Fryer basket.
5. In the heated pan, place butter, lemon juice, garlic, and red pepper flakes and stir to combine.
6. Return the pan to Air Fryer basket.
7. Slide the basket in Air Fryer and select "Air Fry" for 7 minutes.
8. Press "Start/Pause" to begin.
9. After 1 minute of cooking, stir the mixture once.
10. After 2 minutes of cooking, press "Start/Pause" to pause cooking.
11. Remove the basket with pan from Air Fryer and stir in the shrimp, basil, chives and wine.
12. Again, slide the basket in Air Fryer and press "Start/Pause" to resume cooking.
13. While cooking, stir the mixture once after 5 minutes.
14. Remove from Air Fryer and place the pan onto a wire rack for about 1 minute.
15. Stir the mixture and transfer onto serving plates.
16. Serve hot.

Nutritional Information per Serving:

- Calories 333
- Total Fat 18.2 g
- Saturated Fat 10.6 g
- Cholesterol 359 mg
- Sodium 480 mg
- Total Carbs 4.4 g
- Fiber 0.5 g
- Sugar 0.4 g
- Protein 35.1 g

Parmesan Coated Shrimp

Preparation Time: 20 minutes
Cooking Time: 20 minutes
Servings: 6

Ingredients:

- 2/3 cup Parmesan cheese, grated
- 4 garlic cloves, minced
- 2 tablespoons olive oil
- 1 teaspoon dried basil
- ½ teaspoon dried oregano
- 1 teaspoon onion powder
- ½ teaspoon red pepper flakes, crushed
- Ground black pepper, as required
- 2 pounds shrimp, peeled and deveined
- 1-2 tablespoons fresh lemon juice

Method:

1. In a large bowl, mix together the Parmesan cheese, garlic, oil, herbs and spices.
2. Add the shrimp and toss to coat well.
3. Set the temperature of Ninja Max XL Air Fryer to 350 degrees F and select "Air Fry" to preheat for 5 minutes.
4. Press "Start/Pause" to begin.
5. Grease the Air Fryer basket.
6. Arrange half of the shrimp into the prepared Air Fryer basket in a single layer.
7. Slide the basket in Air Fryer and select "Air Fry" for 8-10 minutes.
8. Remove from Air Fryer and transfer the shrimp onto serving plates.
9. Repeat with the remaining shrimp.
10. Drizzle with lemon juice and serve immediately.

Nutritional Information per Serving:

- Calories 258
- Total Fat 9.4 g
- Saturated Fat 2.5 g
- Cholesterol 326 mg
- Sodium 447 mg
- Total Carbs 3.52.1 g
- Fiber 0.2 g
- Sugar 0.2 g
- Protein 38.2 g

Chapter 7: Meat Recipes

Herbed Steak

Preparation Time: 10 minutes
Cooking Time: 15 minutes
Servings: 4

Ingredients:

- 3 garlic cloves, minced
- 1 cup fresh parsley leaves, finely chopped
- 3 tablespoons fresh oregano, finely chopped
- 3 tablespoons fresh mint leaves, finely chopped
- 1 tablespoon ground cumin
- 2 teaspoons smoked paprika
- 1 teaspoon cayenne pepper
- 1 teaspoon red pepper flakes, crushed
- Salt and ground black pepper, as required
- ¾ cup olive oil
- 3 tablespoons red wine vinegar
- 2 (8-ounce) skirt steaks

Method:

1. In a bowl, mix together the garlic, herbs, spices, oil, and vinegar.
2. In a resealable bag, place ¼ cup of the herb mixture and steaks.
3. Seal the bag and shake to coat well.
4. Refrigerate for about 24 hours.
5. Reserve the remaining herb mixture in refrigerator.
6. Remove the steaks from refrigerator and place at room temperature for about 30 minutes.
7. Set the temperature of Ninja Max XL Air Fryer to 390 degrees F and select "Air Fry" to preheat for 5 minutes.
8. Press "Start/Pause" to begin.
9. Grease the Air Fryer basket.
10. Arrange steaks into the prepared Air Fryer basket.
11. Slide the basket in Air Fryer and select "Air Fry" for 10 minutes.
12. Press "Start/Pause" to begin.
13. Remove from Air Fryer and place the steaks onto a cutting board for about 10 minutes before slicing.
14. Cut each steak into desired size slices and transfer onto serving platter.
15. Top with reserved herb mixture and serve.

Nutritional Information per Serving:

- Calories 590
- Total Fat 50.3 g

- Saturated Fat 9.9 g
- Cholesterol 67 mg
- Sodium 100 mg
- Total Carbs 5.8 g

- Fiber 3 g
- Sugar 0.5 g
- Protein 31.8 g

Steak with Bell Peppers

Preparation Time: 15 minutes
Cooking Time: 22 minutes
Servings: 4

Ingredients:

- 1 teaspoon dried oregano, crushed
- 1 teaspoon onion powder
- 1 teaspoon garlic powder
- 1 teaspoon red chili powder
- 1 teaspoon paprika
- Salt, as required
- 1¼ pound flank steak, cut into thin strips
- 3 green bell peppers, seeded and cubed
- 1 red onion, sliced
- 2 tablespoons olive oil
- 3-4 tablespoons feta cheese, crumbled

Method:

1. In a large bowl, mix together the oregano and spices.
2. Add the steak strips, bell peppers, onion, and oil and mix until well combined.
3. Set the temperature of Ninja Max XL Air Fryer to 390 degrees F and select "Air Fry" to preheat for 5 minutes.
4. Press "Start/Pause" to begin.
5. Grease the Air Fryer basket.
6. Arrange half of the steak mixture into the prepared Air Fryer basket.
7. Slide the basket in Air Fryer and select "Air Fry" for 10-11 minutes or until done completely.
8. Press "Start/Pause" to begin.
9. Remove from Air Fryer and transfer the steak mixture onto serving plates.
10. Repeat with the remaining mixture.
11. Serve immediately with the topping of feta.

Nutritional Information per Serving:

- Calories 732
- Total Fat 35 g
- Saturated Fat 12.9 g
- Cholesterol 178 mg
- Sodium 303 mg
- Total Carbs 11.5 g
- Fiber 2.5 g
- Sugar 6.5 g
- Protein 89.3 g

Garlicky Lamb Steaks

Preparation Time: 15 minutes
Cooking Time: 15 minutes
Servings: 4

Ingredients:

- ½ onion, roughly chopped
- 5 garlic cloves, peeled
- 1 tablespoon fresh ginger, peeled
- 1 teaspoon ground fennel
- ½ teaspoon ground cumin
- ½ teaspoon ground cinnamon
- ½ teaspoon cayenne pepper
- Salt and ground black pepper, as required
- 1½ pounds boneless lamb sirloin steaks

Method:

1. In a blender, add the onion, garlic, ginger, and spices and pulse until smooth.
2. Transfer the mixture into a large bowl.
3. Add the lamb steaks and coat with the mixture generously.
4. Refrigerate to marinate for about 24 hours.
5. Set the temperature of Ninja Max XL Air Fryer to 330 degrees F and select "Air Fry" to preheat for 5 minutes.
6. Press "Start/Pause" to begin.
7. Grease the Air Fryer basket.
8. Arrange the steaks into the prepared Air Fryer basket in a single layer.
9. Slide the basket in Air Fryer and select "Air Fry" for 15 minutes, flipping once halfway through.
10. Remove the steaks from Air Fryer and serve.

Nutritional Information per Serving:

- Calories 336
- Total Fat 12.8 g
- Saturated Fat 4.5 g
- Cholesterol 153 mg
- Sodium 171 mg
- Total Carbs 4.2 g
- Fiber 1 g
- Sugar 0.7 g
- Protein 48.4 g

Herbed Beef Roast

Preparation Time: 10 minutes
Cooking Time: 45 minutes
Servings: 6

Ingredients:

- 2 pounds beef roast
- 1 tablespoon olive oil
- 1 teaspoon dried rosemary, crushed
- 1 teaspoon dried thyme, crushed
- 1 teaspoon dried parsley, crushed
- Salt, as required

Method:

1. In a bowl, mix together the oil, herbs, and salt.
2. Coat the roast with herb mixture evenly.
3. Set the temperature of Ninja Max XL Air Fryer to 360 degrees F and select "Air Fry" to preheat for 5 minutes.
4. Press "Start/Pause" to begin.
5. Grease the Air Fryer basket.
6. Arrange the roast into the prepared Air Fryer basket.
7. Slide the basket in Air Fryer and select "Air Fry" for 45 minutes.
8. Press "Start/Pause" to begin.
9. Remove from Air Fryer and transfer the roast onto a platter.
10. With a piece of foil, cover the roast for about 10 minutes before slicing.
11. Cut the roast into desired size slices and serve.

Nutritional Information per Serving:

- Calories 302
- Total Fat 11.8 g
- Saturated Fat 3.9 g
- Cholesterol 135 mg
- Sodium 127 mg
- Total Carbs 0.3 g
- Fiber 0.2 g
- Sugar 0 g
- Protein 45.9 g

Roasted Leg of Lamb

Preparation Time: 10 minutes
Cooking Time: 1 hour 25 minutes
Servings: 4

Ingredients:

- 2 pounds bone-in leg of lamb
- 2 tablespoons olive oil
- Salt and ground black pepper, as required
- 2 fresh rosemary sprigs
- 2 fresh thyme sprigs

Method:

1. Coat the leg of lamb with oil and sprinkle with salt and black pepper.
2. Wrap the leg of lamb with herb sprigs.
3. Set the temperature of Ninja Max XL Air Fryer to 300 degrees F and select "Air Fry" to preheat for 5 minutes.
4. Press "Start/Pause" to begin.
5. Grease the Air Fryer basket.
6. Place leg of lamb into the prepared Air Fryer basket.
7. Slide the basket in Air Fryer and select "Air Fry" for 75 minutes.
8. Remove from Air Fryer and transfer the leg of lamb onto a platter.
9. With a piece of foil, cover the leg of lamb for about 10 minutes before slicing.
10. Cut the leg of lamb into desired size pieces and serve.

Nutritional Information per Serving:

- Calories 493
- Total Fat 24.1 g
- Saturated Fat 7.2 g
- Cholesterol 204 mg
- Sodium 213 mg
- Total Carbs 2.1 g
- Fiber 1.4 g
- Sugar 0 g
- Protein 63.9 g

Crumbed Steak

Preparation Time: 10 minutes
Cooking Time: 10 minutes
Servings: 2

Ingredients:

- 1 cup white flour
- 2 eggs
- 1 cup panko breadcrumbs
- 1 teaspoon garlic powder
- 1 teaspoon onion powder
- Salt and ground black pepper, as required
- 2 (6-ounce) sirloin steaks, pounded slightly

Method:

1. In a shallow bowl, place the flour.
2. Crack the eggs in a second bowl and beat well.
3. In a third bowl, mix together the panko and spices.
4. Coat each steak with the flour, then dip into beaten eggs and finally, coat with panko mixture.
5. Set the temperature of Ninja Max XL Air Fryer to 360 degrees F and select "Air Fry" to preheat for 5 minutes.
6. Press "Start/Pause" to begin.
7. Grease the Air Fryer basket.
8. Arrange steaks into the prepared Air Fryer basket.
9. Slide the basket in Air Fryer and select "Air Fry" for 10 minutes.
10. Press "Start/Pause" to begin.
11. Remove from Air Fryer and transfer the steaks onto the serving plates.
12. Serve immediately.

Nutritional Information per Serving:

- Calories 810
- Total Fat 19.4 g
- Saturated Fat 7 g
- Cholesterol 316 mg
- Sodium 253 mg
- Total Carbs 58.2 g
- Fiber 2.1 g
- Sugar 1.4 g
- Protein 65.4 g

Sausage Pizza

Preparation Time: 15 minutes
Cooking Time: 8 minutes
Serving: 1

Ingredients:

- 1 pita bread
- 1 tablespoon pizza sauce
- 4 pepperoni slices
- ¼ cup cooked sausage, sliced
- 1 tablespoon olives, pitted and sliced
- 1 tablespoon onion, sliced thinly
- ¼ cup mozzarella cheese, shredded
- Pinch of dried thyme
- ¼ teaspoon extra-virgin olive oil

Method:

1. Place the pita bread onto a plate and drizzle with pizza sauce evenly.
2. Arrange the pepperoni slices on top, followed by sausage slices, olives and onion.
3. Sprinkle with the cheese and thyme and then drizzle with oil.
4. Set the temperature of Ninja Max XL Air Fryer to 350 degrees F and select "Air Fry" to preheat for 5 minutes.
5. Press "Start/Pause" to begin.
6. Grease the Air Fryer basket.
7. Arrange the pizza into the prepared Air Fryer basket.
8. Slide the basket in Air Fryer and select "Air Fry" for 8 minutes.
9. Press "Start/Pause" to begin.
10. Remove from Air Fryer and transfer the pizza onto a serving plate.
11. Set aside to cool slightly.
12. Serve warm.

Nutritional Information per Serving:

- Calories 462
- Total Fat 25.2 g
- Saturated Fat 8.1 g
- Cholesterol 60 mg
- Sodium 1100 mg
- Total Carbs 37 g
- Fiber 2.1 g
- Sugar 1.7 g
- Protein 20.7 g

Spiced Pork Chops

Preparation Time: 10 minutes
Cooking Time: 17 minutes
Servings: 2

Ingredients:

- ½ cup panko breadcrumbs
- 1 teaspoon paprika
- ¼ teaspoon garlic powder
- ¼ teaspoon onion powder
- Salt and ground black pepper, as required
- 2 (5-ounce) boneless pork chops, trimmed
- Olive oil cooking spray

Method:

1. In a large shallow bowl, mix together the breadcrumbs and spices.
2. Coat the chops with breadcrumb mixture evenly.
3. Set the temperature of Ninja Max XL Air Fryer to 360 degrees F and select "Air Fry" to preheat for 5 minutes.
4. Press "Start/Pause" to begin.
5. Grease the Air Fryer basket.
6. Arrange the chops into the Air Fryer basket and spray with cooking spray.
7. Slide the basket in Air Fryer and select "Air Fry" for 17 minutes.
8. Press "Start/Pause" to begin.
9. While cooking, flip the chops once halfway through.
10. Remove from Air Fryer and transfer the chops onto serving plates.
11. Serve hot.

Nutritional Information per Serving:

- Calories 305
- Total Fat 7 g
- Saturated Fat 2.5 g
- Cholesterol 103 mg
- Sodium 159 mg
- Total Carbs 5.2 g
- Fiber 0.5 g
- Sugar 0.4 g
- Protein 38.1 g

Pork Meatballs

Preparation Time: 20 minutes
Cooking Time: 24 minutes
Servings: 8

Ingredients:

- 2 pounds ground pork
- 1 medium onion, chopped roughly
- ¼ cup fresh parsley, chopped roughly
- 4 garlic cloves, peeled
- ½ cup feta cheese, crumbled
- ½ cup Italian seasoned breadcrumbs
- 2 eggs, lightly beaten
- 1 tablespoon Worcestershire sauce
- Salt and ground black pepper, as required

Method:

1. In a mini food processor, add the onion, parsley and garlic and pulse until finely chopped.
2. Transfer the onion mixture into a large bowl.
3. Add the remaining ingredients and mix until well combined.
4. Make equal-sized balls from the mixture.
5. Set the temperature of Ninja Max XL Air Fryer to 400 degrees F and select "Air Fry" to preheat for 5 minutes.
6. Press "Start/Pause" to begin.
7. Grease the Air Fryer basket.
8. Arrange half of the meatballs in the prepared Air Fryer basket in a single layer.
9. Slide the basket in Air Fryer and select "Air Fry" for 12 minutes.
10. Press "Start/Pause" to begin.
11. Transfer the meatballs onto a platter.
12. Repeat with remaining meatballs.
13. Serve hot.

Nutritional Information per Serving:

- Calories 242
- Total Fat 7.5 g
- Saturated Fat 3.2 g
- Cholesterol 132 mg
- Sodium 359 mg
- Total Carbs 7.9 g
- Fiber 0.8 g
- Sugar 1.9 g
- Protein 33.8 g

Stuffed Pork Roll

Preparation Time: 20 minutes
Cooking Time: 15 minutes
Servings: 4

Ingredients:

- 1 scallion, chopped
- ¼ cup sun-dried tomatoes, chopped finely
- 2 tablespoons fresh parsley, chopped
- Salt and ground black pepper, as required
- 4 (6-ounce) pork cutlets, pounded slightly
- 2 teaspoons paprika
- ½ tablespoons olive oil

Method:

1. In a bowl, mix together the scallion, tomatoes, parsley, salt, and black pepper.
2. Spread the tomato mixture over each pork cutlet.
3. Roll each cutlet and secure with cocktail sticks.
4. Rub the outer part of rolls with paprika, salt and black pepper.
5. Coat the rolls with oil evenly.
6. Set the temperature of Ninja Max XL Air Fryer to 390 degrees F and select "Air Fry" to preheat for 5 minutes.
7. Press "Start/Pause" to begin.
8. Grease the Air Fryer basket.
9. Arrange pork rolls into the prepared Air Fryer basket in a single layer.
10. Slide the basket in Air Fryer and select "Air Fry" for 15 minutes.
11. Press "Start/Pause" to begin.
12. Remove from Air Fryer and transfer the pork rolls onto serving plates.
13. Serve hot.

Nutritional Information per Serving:

- Calories 244
- Total Fat 14.5 g
- Saturated Fat 2.7 g
- Cholesterol 15 mg
- Sodium 708 mg
- Total Carbs 20.1 g
- Fiber 2.6 g
- Sugar 1.7 g
- Protein 8.2 g

Spicy Roast

Preparation Time: 10 minutes
Cooking Time: 50 minutes
Servings: 8

Ingredients:

- 2½ pounds beef eye of round roast, trimmed
- 2 tablespoons olive oil
- ½ teaspoon onion powder
- ½ teaspoon garlic powder
- ½ teaspoon cayenne pepper
- ½ teaspoon ground black pepper
- Salt, as required

Method:

1. In a bowl, mix together the oil and spices.
2. Coat the roast with spice mixture evenly.
3. Set the temperature of Ninja Max XL Air Fryer to 360 degrees F and select "Air Fry" to preheat for 5 minutes.
4. Press "Start/Pause" to begin.
5. Grease the Air Fryer basket.
6. Arrange roast into the prepared Air Fryer basket.
7. Slide the basket in Air Fryer and select "Air Fry" for 50 minutes.
8. Press "Start/Pause" to begin.
9. Remove from Air Fryer and transfer the roast onto a platter.
10. With a piece of foil, cover the roast for about 10 minutes before slicing.
11. Cut the roast into desired size slices and serve.

Nutritional Information per Serving:

- Calories 261
- Total Fat 9.3 g
- Saturated Fat 2.5 g
- Cholesterol 78 mg
- Sodium 73 mg
- Total Carbs 0.4 g
- Fiber 0.1 g
- Sugar 0.1 g
- Protein 41.7 g

Herbed Pork Chops

Preparation Time: 15 minutes
Cooking Time: 12 minutes
Servings: 3

Ingredients:

- 2 garlic cloves, minced
- ½ tablespoons fresh cilantro, chopped
- ½ tablespoons fresh rosemary, chopped
- ½ tablespoons fresh parsley, chopped
- 2 tablespoons olive oil
- ¾ tablespoons Dijon mustard
- 1 tablespoon ground coriander
- 1 teaspoon sugar
- Salt, as required
- 3 (6-ounce) (1-inch thick) pork chops

Method:

1. In a bowl, mix together the garlic, herbs, oil, mustard, coriander, sugar, and salt.
2. Add the pork chops and coat with marinade generously.
3. Cover the bowl and refrigerate for about 2-3 hours.
4. Remove chops from the refrigerator and set aside at room temperature for about 30 minutes.
5. Set the temperature of Ninja Max XL Air Fryer to 390 degrees F and select "Air Fry" to preheat for 5 minutes.
6. Press "Start/Pause" to begin.
7. Grease the Air Fryer basket.
8. Arrange chops into the prepared Air Fryer basket in a single layer.
9. Slide the basket in Air Fryer and select "Air Fry" for 10-12 minutes.
10. Press "Start/Pause" to begin.
11. Remove from Air Fryer and transfer the chops onto plates.
12. Serve hot.

Nutritional Information per Serving:

- Calories 341
- Total Fat 23.5 g
- Saturated Fat 6.8 g
- Cholesterol 97 mg
- Sodium 535 mg
- Total Carbs 2.9 g
- Fiber 0.4 g
- Sugar 1.4 g
- Protein 32.3 g

Herbed Lamb Chops

Preparation Time: 10 minutes
Cooking Time: 7 minutes
Servings: 2

Ingredients:

- 1 tablespoon fresh lemon juice
- 1 tablespoon olive oil
- 1 teaspoon dried rosemary
- 1 teaspoon dried thyme
- 1 teaspoon dried oregano
- ½ teaspoon ground cumin
- ½ teaspoon ground coriander
- Salt and ground black pepper, as required
- 4 (4-ounce) lamb chops

Method:

1. In a large bowl, mix together the lemon juice, oil, herbs, and spices.
2. Add the chops and coat with the herb mixture evenly.
3. Refrigerate to marinate for about 1 hour
4. Set the temperature of Ninja Max XL Air Fryer to 390 degrees F and select "Air Fry" to preheat for 5 minutes.
5. Press "Start/Pause" to begin.
6. Grease the Air Fryer basket.
7. Arrange chops into the prepared Air Fryer basket in a single layer.
8. Slide the basket in Air Fryer and select "Air Fry" for 7 minutes.
9. While cooking, flip the chops once halfway through.
10. Remove the chops from Air Fryer and transfer onto serving plates.
11. Serve hot.

Nutritional Information per Serving:

- Calories 491
- Total Fat 24 g
- Saturated Fat 7.1 g
- Cholesterol 204 mg
- Sodium 253 mg
- Total Carbs 1.6 g
- Fiber 0.9 g
- Sugar 0.2 g
- Protein 64 g

Almonds Coated Rack of Lamb

Preparation Time: 15 minutes
Cooking Time: 35 minutes
Servings: 5

Ingredients:

- 1 tablespoon olive oil
- 1 garlic clove, minced
- Salt and ground black pepper, as required
- 1 (1¾-pound) rack of lamb
- 1 egg
- 1 tablespoon breadcrumbs
- 3 ounces almonds, finely chopped

Method:

1. In a bowl, mix together the oil, garlic, salt, and black pepper.
2. Coat the rack of lamb evenly with oil mixture.
3. Crack the egg in a shallow bowl and beat well.
4. In another bowl, mix together the breadcrumbs and almonds.
5. Dip the rack of lamb in beaten egg and then, coat with almond mixture.
6. Set the temperature of Ninja Max XL Air Fryer to 220 degrees F and select "Air Fry" to preheat for 5 minutes.
7. Press "Start/Pause" to begin.
8. Grease the Air Fryer basket.
9. Place the rack of lamb into the prepared Air Fryer basket.
10. Slide the basket in Air Fryer and select "Air Fry" for 30 minutes.
11. Press "Start/Pause" to begin.
12. After 30 minutes, set the temperature of to 390 degrees F for 5 minutes.
13. Remove from Air Fryer and place the rack of lamb onto a cutting board for about 5 minutes.
14. With a sharp knife, cut the rack of lamb into individual chops and serve.

Nutritional Information per Serving:

- Calories 408
- Total Fat 26.3 g
- Saturated Fat 6.3 g
- Cholesterol 138 mg
- Sodium 166 mg
- Total Carbs 4.9 g
- Fiber 2.2 g
- Sugar 0.9 g
- Protein 37.2 g

Pesto Rack of Lamb

Preparation Time: 15 minutes
Cooking Time: 15 minutes
Servings: 4

Ingredients:

- ½ bunch fresh mint
- 1 garlic clove
- ¼ cup extra-virgin olive oil
- ½ tablespoons honey
- Salt and ground black pepper, as required
- 1 (1½-pound) rack of lamb

Method:

1. For pesto: in a blender, add the mint, garlic, oil, honey, salt, and black pepper and pulse until smooth.
2. Coat the rack of lamb with pesto evenly.
3. Set the temperature of Ninja Max XL Air Fryer to 200 degrees F and select "Air Fry" to preheat for 5 minutes.
4. Press "Start/Pause" to begin.
5. Grease the Air Fryer basket.
6. Place the rack of lamb into the prepared Air Fryer basket.
7. Slide the basket in Air Fryer and select "Air Fry" for 15 minutes.
8. Press "Start/Pause" to begin.
9. While cooking, coat the rack of lamb with the remaining pesto after every 5 minutes.
10. Remove from Air Fryer and place the rack of lamb onto a cutting board for about 5 minutes.
11. Cut the rack into individual chops and serve.

Nutritional Information per Serving:

- Calories 405
- Total Fat 27.7 g
- Saturated Fat 7.1 g
- Cholesterol 113 mg
- Sodium 161 mg
- Total Carbs 2.8 g
- Fiber 0.3 g
- Sugar 2.2 g
- Protein 34.8 g

Chapter 8: Vegetarian Recipes

Stuffed Bell Peppers

Preparation Time: 15 minutes
Cooking Time: 15 minutes
Servings: 5

Ingredients:

- ½ of small bell pepper, seeded and chopped
- 1 (15-ounce) can diced tomatoes with juice
- 1 (15-ounce) can red kidney beans, rinsed and drained
- 1 cup cooked rice
- 1½ teaspoons Italian seasoning
- 5 large bell peppers, tops removed and seeded
- ½ cup mozzarella cheese, shredded
- 1 tablespoon Parmesan cheese, grated

Method:

1. In a bowl, mix together the chopped bell pepper, tomatoes with juice, beans, rice, and Italian seasoning.
2. Stuff each bell pepper with the rice mixture.
3. Set the temperature of Ninja Max XL Air Fryer to 360 degrees F and select "Air Fry" to preheat for 5 minutes.
4. Press "Start/Pause" to begin.
5. Grease the Air Fryer basket.
6. Arrange the bell peppers into the Air Fryer basket in a single layer.
7. Slide the basket in Air Fryer and select "Air Fry" for 12 minutes.
8. Press "Start/Pause" to begin.
9. Meanwhile, in a bowl, mix together the mozzarella and Parmesan cheese.
10. After 12 minutes of cooking, press "Start/Pause" to pause cooking.
11. Remove the basket from Air Fryer and flip top each bell pepper with cheese mixture.
12. Again, slide the basket in Air Fryer and press "Start/Pause" to resume cooking.
13. Remove from Air Fryer and transfer the bell peppers onto a serving platter.
14. Set aside to cool slightly.
15. Serve warm.

Nutritional Information per Serving:

- Calories 404
- Total Fat 3.4 g
- Saturated Fat 13.4 g
- Cholesterol 183 mg
- Sodium 331 mg
- Total Carbs 2.1 g
- Fiber 0.7 g
- Sugar 10.2 g

- Protein 23.9 g

Glazed Carrots

Preparation Time: 10 minutes
Cooking Time: 12 minutes
Servings: 4

Ingredients:

- 3 cups carrots, peeled and cut into large chunks
- 1 tablespoon olive oil
- 1 tablespoon honey
- 1 tablespoon fresh thyme, finely chopped
- Salt and ground black pepper, as required

Method:

1. Set the temperature of Ninja Max XL Air Fryer to 390 degrees F and select "Air Fry" to preheat for 5 minutes.
2. Press "Start/Pause" to begin.
3. Grease the Air Fryer basket.
4. In a bowl, add the carrot, oil, honey, thyme, salt and black pepper and mix until well combined.
5. Arrange carrot chunks into the prepared Air Fryer basket in a single layer.
6. Slide the basket in Air Fryer and select "Air Fry" for 12 minutes.
7. Press "Start/Pause" to begin.
8. Remove from Air Fryer and transfer the carrot chunks onto serving plates.
9. Serve hot.

Nutritional Information per Serving:

- Calories 82
- Total Fat 3.6 g
- Saturated Fat 0.5 g
- Cholesterol 0 mg
- Sodium 96 mg
- Total Carbs 12.9 g
- Fiber 2.3 g
- Sugar 8.4 g
- Protein 0.8 g

Jacket Potatoes

Preparation Time: 10 minutes
Cooking Time: 15 minutes
Servings: 2

Ingredients:

- 2 potatoes
- 1 tablespoon mozzarella cheese, shredded
- 3 tablespoons sour cream
- 1 tablespoon butter, softened
- 1 teaspoon fresh chives, minced
- Salt and ground black pepper, as required

Method:

1. Set the temperature of Ninja Max XL Air Fryer to 355 degrees F and select "Air Fry" to preheat for 5 minutes.
2. Press "Start/Pause" to begin.
3. Grease the Air Fryer basket.
4. With a fork, prick the potatoes.
5. Arrange potatoes into the prepared Air Fryer basket.
6. Slide the basket in Air Fryer and select "Air Fry" for 15 minutes.
7. Press "Start/Pause" to begin.
8. Meanwhile, in a bowl, add the remaining ingredients and mix until well combined.
9. Remove from Air Fryer and transfer the potatoes onto a platter.
10. Open potatoes from the center and stuff them with cheese mixture.
11. Serve immediately

Nutritional Information per Serving:

- Calories 277
- Total Fat 12.2 g
- Saturated Fat 7.6 g
- Cholesterol 31 mg
- Sodium 226 mg
- Total Carbs 34.8 g
- Fiber 5.1 g
- Sugar 2.5 g
- Protein 8.2 g

Veggie Pizza

Preparation Time: 10 minutes
Cooking Time: 5 minutes
Servings: 1

Ingredients:

- 2 tablespoons marinara sauce
- 1 whole-wheat pita bread
- ½ cup fresh baby spinach leaves
- ½ of small plum tomato, cut into 4 slices
- ½ of garlic clove, sliced thinly
- ½ ounce part-skim mozzarella cheese, shredded
- ½ tablespoon Parmigiano-Reggiano cheese, shredded

Method:

1. Arrange the pita bread onto a plate.
2. Spread marinara sauce over 1 side of each pita bread evenly.
3. Top with the spinach leaves, followed by tomato slices, garlic and cheeses.
4. Set the temperature of Ninja Max XL Air Fryer to 350 degrees F and select "Air Fry" to preheat for 5 minutes.
5. Press "Start/Pause" to begin.
6. Grease the Air Fryer basket.
7. Arrange the pizza into the prepared Air Fryer basket.
8. Slide the basket in Air Fryer and select "Air Fry" for 5 minutes.
9. Press "Start/Pause" to begin.
10. Remove from Air Fryer and transfer the pizza onto a serving plate.
11. Set aside to cool slightly.
12. Serve warm.

Nutritional Information per Serving:

- Calories 266
- Total Fat 6.2 g
- Saturated Fat 2.6 g
- Cholesterol 12 mg
- Sodium 592 mg
- Total Carbs 43.1 g
- Fiber 6.5 g
- Sugar 4.6 g
- Protein 13 g

Zucchini Salad

Preparation Time: 15 minutes
Cooking Time: 30 minutes
Servings: 4

Ingredients:

- 1 pound zucchini, cut into rounds
- 2 tablespoons olive oil
- 1 teaspoon garlic powder
- Salt and ground black pepper, as required
- 5 cups fresh spinach, chopped
- ¼ cup feta cheese, crumbled
- 2 tablespoons fresh lemon juice

Method:

1. Set the temperature of Ninja Max XL Air Fryer to 400 degrees F and select "Air Fry" to preheat for 5 minutes.
2. Press "Start/Pause" to begin.
3. Grease the Air Fryer basket.
4. In a bowl, mix together the zucchini, oil, garlic powder, salt, and black pepper.
5. Arrange zucchini slices into the prepared Air Fryer basket in a single layer.
6. Slide the basket in Air Fryer and select "Air Fry" for 30 minutes.
7. Press "Start/Pause" to begin.
8. While cooking, toss the zucchini slices 3 times after every 8 minutes.
9. Remove from Air Fryer and transfer the zucchini slices onto a plate. Set aside to cool.
10. In a bowl, add the cooked zucchini slices, spinach, feta cheese, lemon juice, a little bit of salt, and black pepper and toss to coat well.
11. Serve immediately.

Nutritional Information per Serving:

- Calories 116
- Total Fat 9.4 g
- Saturated Fat 2.5 g
- Cholesterol 8 mg
- Sodium 186 mg
- Total Carbs 6.2 g
- Fiber 2.2 g
- Sugar 2.8 g
- Protein 4 g

Spiced Eggplant

Preparation Time: 15 minutes
Cooking Time: 27 minutes
Servings: 3

Ingredients:

- 2 medium eggplants, cubed
- 2 tablespoons butter, melted
- 1 tablespoon Maggi seasoning sauce
- 1 teaspoon sumac
- 1 teaspoon garlic powder
- 1 teaspoon onion powder
- Salt and ground black pepper, as required
- 1 tablespoon fresh lemon juice
- 2 tablespoons Parmesan cheese, shredded

Method:

1. Set the temperature of Ninja Max XL Air Fryer to 320 degrees F and select "Air Fry" to preheat for 5 minutes.
2. Press "Start/Pause" to begin.
3. Grease the Air Fryer basket.
4. In a bowl, mix together the eggplant cubes, butter, seasoning sauce and spices.
5. Arrange eggplant cubes into the prepared Air Fryer basket in a single layer.
6. Slide the basket in Air Fryer and select "Air Fry" for 15 minutes.
7. Press "Start/Pause" to begin.
8. Remove from Air Fryer and toss the eggplant cubes.
9. Now, set the temperature of to 350 degrees F for 12 minutes.
10. While cooking, toss the eggplant cubes once halfway through
11. Remove from Air Fryer and transfer the eggplant cubes into a bowl.
12. Add the lemon juice, and Parmesan and toss to coat well.
13. Serve immediately.

Nutritional Information per Serving:

- Calories 180
- Total Fat 9.3 g
- Saturated Fat 5.5 g
- Cholesterol 23 mg
- Sodium 304 mg
- Total Carbs 23 g
- Fiber 13.11.6 g
- Sugar 0 g
- Protein 5.2 g

Pesto Tomatoes

Preparation Time: 15 minutes
Cooking Time: 16 minutes
Servings: 4

Ingredients:

For Pesto:

- ½ cup plus 1 tablespoon olive oil, divided
- 3 tablespoons pine nuts
- Salt, as required
- ½ cup fresh basil, chopped
- ½ cup fresh parsley, chopped
- 1 garlic clove, chopped
- ½ cup Parmesan cheese, grated

For Tomatoes:

- 4 heirloom tomatoes, cut into ½ inch thick slices
- 8 ounces feta cheese, cut into ½ inch thick slices.
- ½ cup red onions, thinly sliced
- 1 tablespoon olive oil
- Salt, as required

Method:

1. Set the temperature of Ninja Max XL Air Fryer to 390 degrees F and select "Air Fry" to preheat for 5 minutes.
2. Press "Start/Pause" to begin.
3. Grease the Air Fryer basket.
4. In a bowl, mix together 1 tablespoon of oil, pine nuts and pinch of salt.
5. Arrange the pine nuts into the prepared Air Fryer basket.
6. Slide the basket in Air Fryer and select "Air Fry" for 2 minutes.
7. Press "Start/Pause" to begin.
8. Remove from Air Fryer and transfer the pine nuts onto a paper towel-lined plate.
9. In a food processor, add the toasted pine nuts, fresh herbs, garlic, Parmesan, and salt and pulse until just combined.
10. While motor is running, slowly add the remaining oil and pulse until smooth.
11. Transfer the pesto into a bowl, and refrigerate, covered until serving.
12. Spread about one tablespoons of pesto onto each tomato slice.
13. Top each tomato slice with one feta and onion slice and drizzle with oil.
14. Again, set the temperature of Ninja Max XL Air Fryer to 390 degrees F and select "Air Fry" to preheat for 5 minutes.
15. Press "Start/Pause" to begin.
16. Grease the Air Fryer basket.
17. Arrange tomato slices into the prepared Air Fryer basket in a single layer.

18. Slide the basket in Air Fryer and select "Air Fry" for 14 minutes.
19. Press "Start/Pause" to begin.
20. Remove from Air Fryer and transfer the tomato slices onto serving plates.
21. Sprinkle with a little salt and serve with the remaining pesto.

Nutritional Information per Serving:

- Calories 616
- Total Fat 56.3 g
- Saturated Fat 18.3 g
- Cholesterol 80 mg
- Sodium 1000 mg
- Total Carbs 12.1 g
- Fiber 2.4 g
- Sugar 6.5 g
- Protein 22.5 g

Cheesy Brussels Sprout

Preparation Time: 15 minutes
Cooking Time: 10 minutes
Servings: 3

Ingredients:

- 1 pound Brussels sprouts, trimmed and halved
- 1 tablespoon balsamic vinegar
- 1 tablespoon extra-virgin olive oil
- Salt and ground black pepper, as required
- ¼ cup whole wheat breadcrumbs
- ¼ cup Parmesan cheese, shredded

Method:

1. Set the temperature of Ninja Max XL Air Fryer to 400 degrees F and select "Air Fry" to preheat for 5 minutes.
2. Press "Start/Pause" to begin.
3. Grease the Air Fryer basket.
4. In a bowl, mix together the Brussels sprouts, vinegar, oil, salt, and black pepper.
5. Arrange Brussels sprouts into the prepared Air Fryer basket in a single layer.
6. Slide the basket in Air Fryer and select "Air Fry" for 10 minutes.
7. Press "Start/Pause" to begin.
8. After 5 minutes of cooking, press "Start/Pause" to pause cooking.
9. Remove the basket from Air Fryer and flip the Brussels sprouts.
10. Sprinkle the Brussels sprouts with breadcrumbs, followed by the cheese.
11. Again, slide the basket in Air Fryer and press "Start/Pause" to resume cooking.
12. Remove from Air Fryer and transfer the Brussels sprouts onto serving plates.
13. Serve hot.

Nutritional Information per Serving:

- Calories 1573
- Total Fat 7.2 g
- Saturated Fat 2 g
- Cholesterol 5 mg
- Sodium 209 mg
- Total Carbs 18.7 g
- Fiber 6.3 g
- Sugar 3.4 g
- Protein 8.7 g

Hasselback Potatoes

Preparation Time: 20 minutes
Cooking Time: 30 minutes
Servings: 4

Ingredients:

- 4 potatoes
- 2 tablespoons olive oil
- 2 tablespoons Parmesan cheese, shredded
- 1 tablespoon fresh chives, chopped

Method:

1. With a sharp knife, cut slits along each potato the short way about ¼-inch apart, making sure slices should stay connected at the bottom.
2. Set the temperature of Ninja Max XL Air Fryer to 355 degrees F and select "Air Fry" to preheat for 5 minutes.
3. Press "Start/Pause" to begin.
4. Grease the Air Fryer basket.
5. Gently brush each potato with oil.
6. Arrange potatoes into the prepared Air Fryer basket.
7. Slide the basket in Air Fryer and select "Air Fry" for 30 minutes.
8. Press "Start/Pause" to begin.
9. After 15 minutes of cooking, press "Start/Pause" to pause cooking.
10. Remove the basket from Air Fryer and coat the potatoes with oil.
11. Again, slide the basket in Air Fryer and press "Start/Pause" to resume cooking.
12. Remove from Air Fryer and transfer the potatoes onto a platter.
13. Garnish with the cheeses, and chives and serve immediately.

Nutritional Information per Serving:

- Calories 207
- Total Fat 7.9 g
- Saturated Fat 1.5 g
- Cholesterol 2 mg
- Sodium 55 mg
- Total Carbs 33.6 g
- Fiber 5.1 g
- Sugar 2.5 g
- Protein 4.6 g

Chickpeas Falafel

Preparation Time: 20 minutes
Cooking Time: 28 minutes
Servings: 6

Ingredients:

- 2 (15-ounce) cans chickpeas, rinsed and drained
- ¼ cup fresh cilantro
- ¼ cup fresh parsley
- 2 garlic cloves, peeled
- 1 large shallot, chopped
- 3 tablespoons all-purpose flour
- 2 tablespoons sesame seeds
- 1 tablespoon fresh lemon juice
- 2 teaspoons ground cumin
- 1 teaspoon paprika
- Salt, as required

Method:

1. In a food processor, add all the ingredients and pulse until mixture comes together in a rough paste.
2. Make about 26 balls from the mixture and then with your fingers, flatten each slightly.
3. Preheat an Air Fryer to 350 degrees F and select "Air Fry" to preheat for 5 minutes.
4. Press "Start/Pause" to begin.
5. Grease the Air Fryer basket.
6. Arrange half of the falafels into the prepared Air Fryer basket in a single layer in 2 batches.
7. Slide the basket in Air Fryer and select "Air Fry" for 14 minutes.
8. Press "Start/Pause" to begin.
9. While cooking, flip the falafels once after 14 minutes.
10. Remove from Air Fryer and transfer the falafels onto serving plates.
11. Repeat with the remaining falafels.
12. Serve warm.

Nutritional Information per Serving:

- Calories 209
- Total Fat 3.4 g
- Saturated Fat 0.4 g
- Cholesterol 0 mg
- Sodium 455 mg
- Total Carbs 37.3 g
- Fiber 7 g
- Sugar 0.2 g
- Protein 8.4 g

Stuffed Tomatoes

Preparation Time: 15 minutes
Cooking Time: 15 minutes
Servings: 2

Ingredients:

- 2 large tomatoes
- ½ cup broccoli, finely chopped
- ½ cup cheddar cheese, shredded
- 1 tablespoon unsalted butter, melted
- ½ teaspoon dried thyme, crushed

Method:

1. Cut the top of each tomato and scoop out pulp and seeds.
2. In a bowl, mix together the chopped broccoli and cheese.
3. Stuff each tomato with broccoli mixture evenly.
4. Set the temperature of Ninja Max XL Air Fryer to 355 degrees F and select "Air Fry" to preheat for 5 minutes.
5. Press "Start/Pause" to begin.
6. Grease the Air Fryer basket.
7. Arrange tomatoes into the prepared Air Fryer basket and drizzle with butter.
8. Slide the basket in Air Fryer and select "Air Fry" for 15 minutes.
9. Press "Start/Pause" to begin.
10. Remove from Air Fryer and transfer the tomatoes onto a serving platter.
11. Set aside to cool slightly.
12. Garnish with thyme and serve.

Nutritional Information per Serving:

- Calories 206
- Total Fat 15.6 g
- Saturated Fat 9.7 g
- Cholesterol 45 mg
- Sodium 233 mg
- Total Carbs 9.1 g
- Fiber 2.9 g
- Sugar 5.3 g
- Protein 9.4 g

Wine Braised Mushrooms

Preparation Time: 15 minutes
Cooking Time: 32 minutes
Servings: 6

Ingredients:

- 1 tablespoon butter
- 2 teaspoons Herbs de Provence
- ½ teaspoon garlic powder
- 2 pounds fresh mushrooms, quartered
- 2 tablespoons white wine

Method:

1. Set the temperature of Ninja Max XL Air Fryer to 320 degrees F and select "Air Fry" to preheat for 5 minutes.
2. Press "Start/Pause" to begin.
3. In the Air Fryer pan, mix together the butter, Herbs de Provence, and garlic powder.
4. Add the mushrooms and stir to combine.
5. Slide the pan in Air Fryer and select "Air Fry" for 30 minutes.
6. Press "Start/Pause" to begin.
7. After 25 minutes of cooking, press "Start/Pause" to pause cooking.
8. Remove the basket from Air Fryer and stir in the wine.
9. Again, slide the basket in Air Fryer and press "Start/Pause" to resume cooking.
10. Remove from Air Fryer and transfer the mushrooms onto serving plates.
11. Serve hot.

Nutritional Information per Serving:

- Calories 54
- Total Fat 2.4 g
- Saturated Fat 1.2 g
- Cholesterol 5 mg
- Sodium 123 mg
- Total Carbs 5.3 g
- Fiber 1.5 g
- Sugar 2.7 g
- Protein 4.8 g

Cheesy Mushrooms

Preparation Time: 15 minutes
Cooking Time: 6 minutes
Servings: 2

Ingredients:

- 2 Portobello mushroom caps, stemmed
- 2 tablespoons olive oil
- 1/8 teaspoon dried Italian seasonings
- Salt, as required
- 2 tablespoons canned tomatoes, chopped
- 2 tablespoons mozzarella cheese, shredded
- 2 Kalamata olives, pitted and sliced
- 2 tablespoons Parmesan cheese, grated freshly
- 1 teaspoon red pepper flakes, crushed

Method:

1. Set the temperature of Ninja Max XL Air Fryer to 320 degrees F and select "Air Fry" to preheat for 5 minutes.
2. Press "Start/Pause" to begin.
3. Grease the Air Fryer basket.
4. With a spoon, scoop out the center of each mushroom cap.
5. Coat each mushroom cap with oil from both sides.
6. Sprinkle the inside of caps with Italian seasoning and salt.
7. Place the tomato pieces over both caps, followed by the olives and mozzarella cheese.
8. Arrange mushroom caps into the prepared Air Fryer basket.
9. Slide the basket in Air Fryer and select "Air Fry" for 6 minutes.
10. Press "Start/Pause" to begin.
11. Remove from Air Fryer and immediately sprinkle with the Parmesan cheese and red pepper flakes.
12. Serve immediately.

Nutritional Information per Serving:

- Calories 132
- Total Fat 6.9 g
- Saturated Fat 3.7 g
- Cholesterol 19 mg
- Sodium 330 mg
- Total Carbs 5.8 g
- Fiber 1.7 g
- Sugar 0.4 g
- Protein 13.8 g

Veggie Rice

Preparation Time: 15 minutes
Cooking Time: 18 minutes
Servings: 2

Ingredients:

- 2 cups cooked white rice
- 1 tablespoon vegetable oil
- 2 teaspoons sesame oil, toasted and divided
- 1 tablespoon water
- Salt and ground white pepper, as required
- 1 large egg, lightly beaten
- ½ cup frozen peas, thawed
- ½ cup frozen carrots, thawed
- 1 teaspoon soy sauce
- 1 teaspoon Sriracha sauce
- ½ teaspoon sesame seeds, toasted

Method:

1. In a large bowl, add the rice, vegetable oil, one teaspoon of sesame oil, water, salt, and white pepper and mix well.
2. Set the temperature of Ninja Max XL Air Fryer to 380 degrees F and select "Air Fry" to preheat for 5 minutes.
3. Press "Start/Pause" to begin.
4. Lightly, grease the Air Fryer pan.
5. Transfer rice mixture into the prepared Air Fryer pan.
6. Slide the basket in Air Fryer and select "Air Fry" for 18 minutes.
7. Press "Start/Pause" to begin.
8. While cooking, stir the mixture once after 12 minutes.
9. After 12 minutes of cooking, press "Start/Pause" to pause cooking.
10. Remove the pan from Air Fryer and place the beaten egg over rice.
11. Again, slide the basket in Air Fryer and press "Start/Pause" to resume cooking.
12. After 16 minutes of cooking, press "Start/Pause" to pause cooking.
13. Remove the basket from Air Fryer and stir in the peas and carrots.
14. Again, slide the basket in Air Fryer and press "Start/Pause" to resume cooking.
15. Meanwhile, in a bowl, mix together the soy sauce, Sriracha sauce, sesame seeds and the remaining sesame oil.
16. Remove from Air Fryer and transfer the rice mixture into a serving bowl.
17. Drizzle with the sauce mixture and serve.

Nutritional Information per Serving:

- Calories 443
- Total Fat 16.4 g
- Saturated Fat 3.2 g
- Cholesterol 95mg

- Sodium 329 mg
- Total Carbs 62.3 g
- Fiber 3.6 g

- Sugar 3.6 g
- Protein 10.1 g

Broccoli with Olives

Preparation Time: 15 minutes
Cooking Time: 19 minutes
Servings: 6

Ingredients:

- 2 pounds broccoli, stemmed and cut into 1-inch florets
- 2 tablespoons olive oil
- Salt and ground black pepper, as required
- 1/3 cup Kalamata olives, halved and pitted
- 2 teaspoons fresh lemon zest, grated
- ¼ cup Parmesan cheese, grated

Method:

1. In a pan of the boiling water, add the broccoli and cook for about 3-4 minutes.
2. Drain the broccoli well.
3. Set the temperature of Ninja Max XL Air Fryer to 400 degrees F and select "Air Fry" to preheat for 5 minutes.
4. Press "Start/Pause" to begin.
5. Grease the Air Fryer basket.
6. In a bowl, mix together the broccoli, oil, salt, and black pepper.
7. Arrange the broccoli florets into the prepared Air Fryer basket.
8. Slide the basket in Air Fryer and select "Air Fry" for 15 minutes.
9. Press "Start/Pause" to begin.
10. While cooking, toss the broccoli florets once halfway through.
11. Remove from Air Fryer and immediately stir in the olives, lemon zest and cheese.
12. Serve immediately.

Nutritional Information per Serving:

- Calories 141
- Total Fat 8.6 g
- Saturated Fat 2.5 g
- Cholesterol 10 mg
- Sodium 395 mg
- Total Carbs 11.3 g
- Fiber 4.2 g
- Sugar 2.6 g
- Protein 8.3 g

Chapter 9: Dessert Recipes

Strawberry Cupcakes

Preparation Time: 15 minutes
Cooking Time: 8 minutes
Servings: 10

Ingredients:

For Cupcakes:

- ½ cup caster sugar
- 7 tablespoons butter
- 2 eggs
- ½ teaspoon vanilla essence
- 7/8 cup self-rising flour

For Frosting:

- 1 cup icing sugar
- 3½ tablespoons butter
- 1 tablespoon whipped cream
- ¼ cup fresh strawberries, pureed
- ½ teaspoon pink food color

Method:

1. In a bowl, add butter, and sugar and beat until fluffy and light.
2. Then, add the eggs, one at a time and beat until well combined.
3. Stir in the vanilla extract.
4. Gradually, add the flour beating continuously until well combined.
5. Place the mixture into silicon cups.
6. Set the temperature of Ninja Max XL Air Fryer to 340 degrees F and select "Air Fry" to preheat for 5 minutes.
7. Press "Start/Pause" to begin.
8. Arrange the silicon cups into the Air Fryer basket.
9. Slide the basket in Air Fryer and select "Air Fry" for 8 minutes.
10. Press "Start/Pause" to begin.
11. Remove the silicon cups from Air Fryer and place onto a wire rack to cool for about 10 minutes.
12. Now, invert the cupcakes onto wire rack to completely cool before frosting.
13. For frosting: in a bowl, add the icing sugar, and butter and beat until fluffy and light.
14. Add the whipped cream, strawberry puree, and color. Mix until well combined.
15. Fill the pastry bag with icing and decorate the cupcakes.

Nutritional Information per Serving:

- Calories 250
- Total Fat 13.6 g
- Saturated Fat 8.2 g
- Cholesterol 66 mg
- Sodium 99 mg

- Total Carbs 30.7 g
- Fiber 0.4 g
- Sugar 0 g
- Protein 22.1 g

Cookie Dough Bites

Preparation Time: 15 minutes
Cooking Time: 20 minutes
Servings: 6

Ingredients:

- 16½ ounces store-bought chilled chocolate chip cookie dough
- ¼ cup butter, melted
- ½ cup chocolate cookie crumbs
- 2 tablespoons sugar

Method:

1. Cut the cookie dough into 12 equal-sized pieces and then, shape each into a ball.
2. In a shallow dish, place the melted butter.
3. In another dish, mix together the cookie crumbs, and sugar.
4. Dip each cookie ball in the melted butter and then evenly coat with the cookie crumbs.
5. In the bottom of a baking sheet, place the coated cookie balls and freeze for at least 2 hours.
6. Preheat the Air Fryer to 350 degrees F and select "Air Fry" to preheat for 5 minutes.
7. Press "Start/Pause" to begin.
8. Line the Air Fryer basket with a piece of foil.
9. Place the cookies balls in the Air Fryer basket in a single layer in 2 batches.
10. Slide the basket in Air Fryer and select "Air Fry" for 10 minutes.
11. Press "Start/Pause" to begin.
12. Remove from Air Fryer and serve warm.

Nutritional Information per Serving:

- Calories 383
- Total Fat 21.5 g
- Saturated Fat 9 g
- Cholesterol 41 mg
- Sodium 334 mg
- Total Carbs 48.6 g
- Fiber 2.6 g
- Sugar 29.2 g
- Protein 2.9 g

Stuffed Apples

Preparation Time: 15 minutes
Cooking Time: 13 minutes
Servings: 4

Ingredients:

For Stuffed Apples

- 4 small firm apples, cored
- ½ cup golden raisins

For Vanilla Sauce

- ½ cup whipped cream
- 2 tablespoons sugar

- ½ cup blanched almonds
- 2 tablespoons sugar

- ½ teaspoon vanilla extract

Method:

1. In a food processor, add the raisins, almonds, and sugar and pulse until chopped.
2. Carefully, stuff each apple with raisin mixture.
3. Set the temperature of Ninja Max XL Air Fryer to 355 degrees F and select "Air Fry" to preheat for 5 minutes.
4. Press "Start/Pause" to begin.
5. Line a baking dish with a parchment paper.
6. Place apples into the prepared baking dish.
7. Arrange the baking dish into the Air Fryer basket.
8. Slide the basket in Air Fryer and select "Air Fry" for 10 minutes.
9. Press "Start/Pause" to begin.
10. Meanwhile, for vanilla sauce: in a pan, add the cream, sugar, and vanilla extract over medium heat and cook for about 2-3 minutes or until sugar is dissolved, stirring continuously.
11. Remove the baking dish from Air Fryer and transfer the apples onto plates to cool slightly
12. Top with the vanilla sauce and serve.

Nutritional Information per Serving:

- Calories 329
- Total Fat 11.1 g
- Saturated Fat 3.4 g
- Cholesterol 17 mg
- Sodium 9 mg

- Total Carbs 60.2 g
- Fiber 7.6 g
- Sugar 46.5 g
- Protein 4 g

Chocolate Muffins

Preparation Time: 20 minutes
Cooking Time: 30 minutes
Servings: 12

Ingredients:

- 1 1/3 cups self-rising flour
- 2/3 cup plus 3 tablespoons caster sugar
- 2½ tablespoons cocoa powder
- 3½ ounces butter
- 5 tablespoons milk
- 2 medium eggs
- ½ teaspoon vanilla extract
- Water, as required
- ½ ounce milk chocolate, finely chopped

Method:

1. In a bowl, mix well flour, sugar, and cocoa powder.
2. With a pastry cutter, cut in the butter until a breadcrumb like mixture forms.
3. In another bowl, mix together the milk, and eggs.
4. Add the egg mixture into flour mixture and mix until well combined.
5. Add the vanilla extract and a little water and mix until well combined.
6. Fold in the chopped chocolate.
7. Set the temperature of Ninja Max XL Air Fryer to 355 degrees F and select "Air Fry" to preheat for 5 minutes.
8. Press "Start/Pause" to begin.
9. Grease 12 muffin molds.
10. Transfer mixture evenly into the prepared muffin molds.
11. Arrange the molds into the Air Fryer basket in 2 batches.
12. Slide the basket in Air Fryer and select "Air Fry" for 9 minutes.
13. Press "Start/Pause" to begin.
14. After 9 minutes of cooking, set the temperature to 320 degrees F for 6 minutes.
15. Remove the muffin molds from Air Fryer and place onto a wire rack to cool for about 10 minutes.
16. Now, invert the muffins onto the wire rack to cool completely before serving.

Nutritional Information per Serving:

- Calories 389
- Total Fat 31.2 g
- Saturated Fat 19.5 g
- Cholesterol 107 mg
- Sodium 226 mg
- Total Carbs 26.3 g
- Fiber 0.8 g
- Sugar 15.1 g
- Protein 3.2 g

Chocolate Cheesecake

Preparation Time: 20 minutes
Cooking Time: 34 minutes
Servings: 6

Ingredients:

- 3 eggs, whites and yolks separated
- 1 cup white chocolate, chopped
- ½ cup cream cheese, softened
- 2 tablespoons cocoa powder
- 2 tablespoons powdered sugar
- ¼ cup apricot jam

Method:

1. In a bowl, add the egg whites and refrigerate to chill before using.
2. In a microwave-safe bowl, add the chocolate and microwave on high heat for about 2 minutes, stirring after every 30 seconds.
3. In the bowl of chocolate, add the cream cheese and microwave for about 1-2 minutes or until cream cheese melts completely.
4. Remove from microwave and stir in cocoa powder and egg yolks.
5. Remove the egg whites from refrigerator and beat until firm peaks form.
6. Add 1/3 of the whipped egg whites into cheese mixture and gently, stir to combine.
7. Fold in the remaining egg whites.
8. Set the temperature of Ninja Max XL Air Fryer to 285 degrees F and select "Air Fry" to preheat for 5 minutes.
9. Press "Start/Pause" to begin.
10. Arrange the cake pan into the Air Fryer basket.
11. Slide the basket in Air Fryer and select "Air Fry" for 30 minutes.
12. Press "Start/Pause" to begin.
13. Remove from the Air Fryer and set aside to cool completely.
14. Refrigerate to chill before serving.
15. Just before serving, dust with the powdered sugar and spread the jam on top evenly.
16. Cut into desired sized slices and serve.

Nutritional Information per Serving:

- Calories 298
- Total Fat 18.3 g
- Saturated Fat 10.6 g
- Cholesterol 109 mg
- Sodium 119 mg
- Total Carbs 29.7 g
- Fiber 0.6 g
- Sugar 25.4 g
- Protein 6.3 g

Fried Banana Slices

Preparation Time: 15 minutes
Cooking Time: 15 minutes
Servings: 8

Ingredients:

- 4 medium ripe bananas, peeled
- 1/3 cup rice flour, divided
- 2 tablespoons all-purpose flour
- 2 tablespoons cornflour
- 2 tablespoons desiccated coconut
- ½ teaspoon baking powder
- ½ teaspoon ground cardamom
- Pinch of salt
- Water, as required
- ¼ cup sesame seeds

Method:

1. In a shallow bowl, mix well 2 tablespoons of rice flour, all-purpose flour, corn flour, coconut, baking powder, cardamom, and salt.
2. Gradually, add enough water and mix until a thick and smooth mixture forms.
3. In a second bowl, place the remaining rice flour.
4. In a third bowl, place the sesame seeds.
5. Cut each banana into half and then, cut each half in 2 pieces lengthwise.
6. Dip the banana slices into coconut mixture and then, coat with the remaining rice flour, followed by the sesame seeds.
7. Set the temperature of Ninja Max XL Air Fryer to 392 degrees F and select "Air Fry" to preheat for 5 minutes.
8. Press "Start/Pause" to begin.
9. Line the Air Fryer basket with a greased and floured piece of foil.
10. Arrange banana slices into the prepared Air Fryer basket in a single layer.
11. Slide the basket in Air Fryer and select "Air Fry" for 15 minutes.
12. Press "Start/Pause" to begin.
13. While cooking, flip the banana slices once halfway through.
14. Remove from Air Fryer and transfer the banana slices onto plates to cool slightly
15. Serve warm.

Nutritional Information per Serving:

- Calories 122
- Total Fat 2.9 g
- Saturated Fat 0.7 g
- Cholesterol 0 mg
- Sodium 24 mg
- Total Carbs 23.6 g
- Fiber 2.6 g
- Sugar 7.7 g
- Protein 2.2 g

Pineapple Bites

Preparation Time: 15 minutes
Cooking Time: 10 minutes
Servings: 4

Ingredients:

For Pineapple Sticks:

- ½ of pineapple
- ¼ cup desiccated coconut

For Yogurt Dip:

- 1 tablespoon fresh mint leaves, minced
- 1 cup vanilla yogurt

Method:

1. With a sharp knife, remove the outer peel of pineapple and then, cut into 1-2 inch thick sticks lengthwise.
2. Add the desiccated coconut in a shallow dish.
3. Coat the pineapple sticks evenly with coconut.
4. Set the temperature of Ninja Max XL Air Fryer to 390 degrees F and select "Air Fry" to preheat for 5 minutes.
5. Press "Start/Pause" to begin.
6. Place the pineapple sticks in the Air Fryer basket in a single layer.
7. Slide the basket in Air Fryer and select "Air Fry" for 10 minutes.
8. Press "Start/Pause" to begin.
9. For dip: in a bowl, mix together the mint, and yogurt.
10. Remove from Air Fryer and transfer the pineapple sticks onto a platter.
11. Serve the pineapple sticks with yogurt dip.

Nutritional Information per Serving:

- Calories 127
- Total Fat 2.2 g
- Saturated Fat 1.8 g
- Cholesterol 4 mg
- Sodium 58 mg
- Total Carbs 23.2 g
- Fiber 2.3 g
- Sugar 18.3 g
- Protein 4.4 g

Fruity Crumble

Preparation Time: 15 minutes
Cooking Time: 20 minutes
Servings: 4

Ingredients:

- ½ pound fresh apricots, pitted and cubed
- 1 cup fresh blackberries
- 1/3 cup sugar, divided
- 1 tablespoon fresh lemon juice
- 7/8 cup flour
- Pinch of salt
- 1 tablespoon cold water
- ¼ cup chilled butter, cubed

Method:

1. Set the temperature of Ninja Max XL Air Fryer to 390 degrees F and select "Air Fry" to preheat for 5 minutes.
2. Press "Start/Pause" to begin.
3. Grease a baking pan.
4. In a large bowl, mix together the apricots, blackberries, 2 tablespoons of sugar, and lemon juice.
5. In another bowl, add the flour, remaining sugar, salt, water, and butter. Mix until a crumbly mixture forms.
6. Place the apricot mixture into the prepared baking pan and top with the flour mixture evenly.
7. Place the pan in the Air Fryer basket.
8. Slide the basket in Air Fryer and select "Air Fry" for 20 minutes.
9. Press "Start/Pause" to begin.
10. Remove the baking pan from Air Fryer and place onto a wire rack to cool for about 10 minutes.
11. Serve warm.

Nutritional Information per Serving:

- Calories 307
- Total Fat 12.4 g
- Saturated Fat 7.4 g
- Cholesterol 31 mg
- Sodium 123 mg
- Total Carbs 47.3 g
- Fiber 3.8 g
- Sugar 23.7 g
- Protein 4.2g

Chocolate Soufflé

Preparation Time: 10 minutes
Cooking Time: 16 minutes
Servings: 2

Ingredients:

- 3 ounces semi-sweet chocolate, chopped
- ¼ cup butter
- 2 eggs, egg yolks and whites separated
- 3 tablespoons sugar
- ½ teaspoon pure vanilla extract
- 2 tablespoons all-purpose flour
- 1 teaspoon powdered sugar plus extra for dusting

Method:

1. In a microwave-safe bowl, put the butter, and chocolate and microwave on high heat for about 2 minutes or until melted completely, stirring after every 30 seconds.
2. Remove from microwave and stir the mixture until smooth.
3. In another bowl, add the egg yolks and beat well.
4. Add the sugar, and vanilla extract and beat well.
5. Add the chocolate mixture and mix until well combined.
6. Add the flour and mix well.
7. In a clean glass bowl, add the egg whites and beat until soft peaks form.
8. Fold the whipped egg whites in 3 portions into the chocolate mixture.
9. Set the temperature of Ninja Max XL Air Fryer to 330 degrees F and select "Air Fry" to preheat for 5 minutes.
10. Press "Start/Pause" to begin.
11. Grease 2 ramekins and sprinkle each with a pinch of sugar.
12. Place mixture evenly into the prepared ramekins and with the back of a spoon, smooth the top surface.
13. Arrange the ramekins into the Air Fryer basket.
14. Slide the basket in Air Fryer and select "Air Fry" for 14 minutes.
15. Press "Start/Pause" to begin.
16. Remove from Air Fryer and set aside to cool slightly.
17. Sprinkle with the powdered sugar and serve warm.

Nutritional Information per Serving:

- Calories 595
- Total Fat 38.7 g
- Saturated Fat 23 g
- Cholesterol 225 mg
- Sodium 225 mg
- Total Carbs 53.9 g
- Fiber 0.2 g
- Sugar 42.3 g
- Protein 9.4 g

Fudge Brownie

Preparation Time: 15 minutes
Cooking Time: 20 minutes
Servings: 8

Ingredients:

- 1 cup sugar
- ½ cup butter, melted
- ½ cup flour
- 1/3 cup cocoa powder
- 1 teaspoon baking powder
- 2 eggs
- 1 teaspoon vanilla extract

Method:

1. In a large bowl, add the sugar, and butter and beat until light and fluffy.
2. Add the remaining ingredients and mix until well combined.
3. Set the temperature of Ninja Max XL Air Fryer to 350 degrees F and select "Air Fry" to preheat for 5 minutes.
4. Press "Start/Pause" to begin.
5. Grease a baking pan.
6. Place mixture into the prepared pan evenly and with the back of spatula, smooth the top surface.
7. Arrange the baking pan into the Air Fryer basket.
8. Slide the basket in Air Fryer and select "Air Fry" for 20 minutes.
9. Press "Start/Pause" to begin.
10. Remove the baking pan from Air Fryer and set aside to cool completely.
11. Cut into 8 equal-sized squares and serve.

Nutritional Information per Serving:

- Calories 250
- Total Fat 13.2 g
- Saturated Fat 7.9 g
- Cholesterol 71 mg
- Sodium 99 mg
- Total Carbs 33.4 g
- Fiber 1.3 g
- Sugar 25.2 g
- Protein 3 g

Chocolate Pudding

Preparation Time: 15 minutes
Cooking Time: 14 minutes
Servings: 4

Ingredients:

- ½ cup butter
- 2/3 cup dark chocolate, chopped
- ¼ cup caster sugar
- 2 medium eggs
- 2 teaspoons fresh orange rind, finely grated
- ¼ cup fresh orange juice
- 2 tablespoons self-rising flour

Method:

1. In a microwave-safe bowl, add the butter, and chocolate and microwave on high heat for about 2 minutes or until melted completely, stirring after every 30 seconds.
2. Remove from microwave and stir the mixture until smooth.
3. Add the sugar, and eggs and beat until frothy.
4. Add the orange rind and juice, followed by flour and mix until well combined.
5. Set the temperature of Ninja Max XL Air Fryer to 355 degrees F and select "Air Fry" to preheat for 5 minutes.
6. Press "Start/Pause" to begin.
7. Grease 4 ramekins.
8. Divide mixture into the prepared ramekins about ¾ full.
9. Arrange the ramekins into the Air Fryer basket.
10. Slide the basket in Air Fryer and select "Air Fry" for 12 minutes.
11. Press "Start/Pause" to begin.
12. Remove from the Air Fryer and set aside to completely cool before serving.
13. Serve warm.

Nutritional Information per Serving:

- Calories 454
- Total Fat 33.6 g
- Saturated Fat 21.1 g
- Cholesterol 149 mg
- Sodium 217 mg
- Total Carbs 34.2 g
- Fiber 1.2 g
- Sugar 28.4 g
- Protein 5.7 g

Apple Bread Pudding

Preparation Time: 15 minutes
Cooking Time: 44 minutes
Servings: 8

Ingredients:

For Bread Pudding:

- 10½ ounces bread, cubed
- ½ cup apple, peeled, cored and chopped
- ½ cup raisins
- ¼ cup walnuts, chopped
- 1½ cups milk
- ¾ cup water
- 5 tablespoons honey
- 2 teaspoons ground cinnamon
- 2 teaspoons cornstarch
- 1 teaspoon vanilla extract

For Topping:

- 1 1/3 cups plain flour
- 3/5 cup brown sugar
- 7 tablespoons butter

Method:

1. In a large bowl, mix together the bread, apple, raisins, and walnuts.
2. In another bowl, add the remaining pudding ingredients and mix until well combined.
3. Add the milk mixture into bread mixture and mix until well combined.
4. Refrigerate for about 15 minutes, tossing occasionally.
5. For topping: in a bowl, mix together the flour and sugar.
6. With a pastry cutter, cut in the butter until a crumbly mixture forms.
7. Set the temperature of Ninja Max XL Air Fryer to 355 degrees F and select "Air Fry" to preheat for 5 minutes.
8. Press "Start/Pause" to begin.
9. Place the mixture evenly into 2 baking pans and spread the topping mixture on top of each.
10. Place 1 pan into the Air Fryer basket.
11. Slide the basket in Air Fryer and select "Air Fry" for 22 minutes.
12. Press "Start/Pause" to begin.
13. Repeat with the remaining pan.
14. Remove from the Air Fryer and serve warm.

Nutritional Information per Serving:

- Calories 432
- Total Fat 14.8 g

- Saturated Fat 7.4 g
- Cholesterol 30 mg
- Sodium 353 mg
- Total Carbs 69.1 g

- Fiber 2.8 g
- Sugar 32 g
- Protein 7.9 g

Fruity Tacos

Preparation Time: 10 minutes
Cooking Time: 5 minutes
Servings: 2

Ingredients:

- 2 soft shell tortillas
- 4 tablespoons strawberry jelly
- ¼ cup blueberries
- ¼ cup raspberries
- 2 tablespoons powdered sugar

Method:

1. Set the temperature of Ninja Max XL Air Fryer to 300 degrees F and select "Air Fry" to preheat for 5 minutes.
2. Press "Start/Pause" to begin.
3. Lightly, grease the Air Fryer basket.
4. Arrange the tortillas onto a smooth surface.
5. Spread two tablespoons of strawberry jelly over each tortilla and top each with berries.
6. Sprinkle each with the powdered sugar.
7. Arrange tortillas into the prepared Air Fryer basket.
8. Slide the basket in Air Fryer and select "Air Fry" for 5 minutes.
9. Press "Start/Pause" to begin.
10. Remove from the Air Fryer and transfer the tortillas onto a platter.
11. Serve warm.

Nutritional Information per Serving:

- Calories 202
- Total Fat 0.9 g
- Saturated Fat 0.1 g
- Cholesterol 0 mg
- Sodium 11 mg
- Total Carbs 49.2 g
- Fiber 3 g
- Sugar 34.5 g
- Protein 1.7 g

Conclusion

Air fryers have become extremely popular in the last few years due to their ease of use, their speed, and the healthier foods they produce. Preparing your favorite meals in record time with little cleanup has never been easier with Ninja air fryer. This Cookbook shows you how to do it all seamlessly, step by step, it gives you best tips and offers up a wide variety of delicious dishes, from air fryer classics to unexpected additions. Ninja air fryer will help you make quick and delicious meals, save time in the kitchen, and enjoy the family!

www.ingramcontent.com/pod-product-compliance
Lightning Source LLC
Chambersburg PA
CBHW050636150426
42811CB00052B/848